COMPUTER SIMULATION APPLICATIONS

Applied Social Research Methods Series
Volume 25

APPLIED SOCIAL RESEARCH
METHODS SERIES

Series Editors:
LEONARD BICKMAN, Peabody College, Vanderbilt University, Nashville
DEBRA J. ROG, Vanderbilt University, Washington, DC

COMPUTER SIMULATION APPLICATIONS

An Introduction

Marcia Lynn Whicker
Lee Sigelman

Applied Social Research Methods Series
Volume 25

SAGE PUBLICATIONS
The International Professional Publishers
Newbury Park   London   New Delhi

For information address:

SAGE Publications, Inc.
2455 Teller Road
Newbury Park, California 91320

SAGE Publications Ltd.
6 Bonhill Street
London EC2A 4PU
England

SAGE Publications India Pvt. Ltd.
M-32 Market
Greater Kailash I
New Delhi 110 048 India

Printed in the United States of America

Library of Congress Cataloging-in-Publication Data

Whicker, Marcia Lynn.
    Computer simulation applications : an introduction / Marcia Lynn
Whicker, Lee Sigelman.
        p.   cm. — (Applied social research methods series ; v. 25)
    Includes bibliographical references.
    ISBN 0-8039-3245-6. — ISBN 0-8039-3246-4 (pbk.)
    1. Computer simulation.   I. Sigelman, Lee.   II. Title.
III. Series.
QA76.9.C65W49   1991
003′3—dc20   90-25980
                                                                    CIP

FIRST PRINTING, 1991

Sage Production Editor: Astrid Virding

Contents

1

Thinking About Simulation: The Pieces That Make the Whole

Simulation is an activity in which we all engage every day of our lives. When small children play cowboy, or when students or their teachers try to appear more knowledgeable about a subject than they really are, or when elderly people think back to "what might have been" in their lives, they are all simulating, whether they know it or not. Their conscious and unconscious reasons for engaging in this type of activity are infinitely varied, but no matter what these reasons may be, they are all using their imaginations to invent an "alternate reality." Sometimes people allow their imaginations to run wild and escape to an alternate reality that bears little resemblance to the real world they actually inhabit. At other times, they stay as firmly anchored in reality as they possibly can, trying, for example, to imagine how they will perform in a situation that they know is about to occur.

When some X (e.g., a small child, a teacher, or an elderly person) assumes the role of some Y (e.g., a cowboy, an expert, or a young person facing an important decision), we say that X simulates Y. When an actor successfully portrays Hamlet, the audience's attention is riveted upon the actor's rendition of the character, not on the actor *per se*. In simulation it is the Y upon which true interest focuses, but for one reason or another Y itself cannot be directly experienced or observed; children, after all, are not really Old West gunfighters, and elderly people cannot really relive their lives.

A simulation model (X) assumes meaning and importance primarily by virtue of its similarity to some phenomenon of interest (Y). This similarity might be physical. Indeed, this is the sense in which we speak of building a "model airplane" (a miniature representation of a full-sized plane), and it is also the sense in which a person who fits the prevailing notion of physical attractiveness may decide to pursue a career as a "model." Physical similarity, however, is not the only, or even necessarily the most important, dimension of likeness between the model and the phenomenon being modeled. Often, *conceptual* similarity—a likeness of ideas—is the key component of a useful simulation (Barton, 1970), with physical similarity making very little difference.

1

Simulation is common not only in everyday life, but also in science, including social science; so common, we believe, that it is easy to lose sight of its importance. To be sure, much scientific work is fairly cut-and-dried; laboratory-based scientists, for example, spend a great deal of their time carrying out carefully controlled experiments, painstakingly recording the results, and conducting standard statistical tests of these results. Activities of this sort proceed according to "the book," and provide relatively little leeway for the free play of the imagination. But it would be a mistake to conclude that science is the province of the dull and unimaginative. Scientific analysis begins, in effect, as a "what if?" question. For a chemist, the question might be "If we combined these two gasses, which have never been combined before, what would the reaction be?" For an anthropologist, it might be "What would happen to the system of interpersonal relations in a given culture if a new medium of economic exchange were introduced?" Facing questions of this nature, which may stem from the theoretical structure of a field, from pressing public policy concerns, from idle curiosity, or from a vast array of other sources, a scientist would proceed by considering what various theories predict about the outcome and then by undertaking a test of how accurate these predictions appear to be.

So simulation, in the broad sense of using one's imagination to ask "what if?" questions, fundamentally shapes scientific work by helping define the questions scientists ask. Unfortunately, we claim no expertise with regard to teaching simulation, thus understood, and we would be skeptical about the promises of anyone who does claim such expertise, for we know of no way to instruct someone how to be imaginative, let alone usefully imaginative.

Why, in light of this disclaimer, should the reader proceed any further? Since our subject is *computer* simulation, is it possible that the computer can teach what we ourselves cannot? Not really, for imaginativeness and the ability to impart it are not numbered among the computer's many impressive capabilities. In this book, we focus on simulation less as a means of posing questions than as a means of deriving answers. The real value of simulation is not that it permits us to ask better (more important, more imaginative, and so on) questions, but that it provides a means of deriving, in at least a preliminary manner, answers that would not be available if we relied on more commonplace methods of data acquisition and analysis. Mastery of simulation techniques and, more broadly, adoption of a simulation orientation, can add an important set of tools to the ability of social scientists to address issues that concern them.

It is well to emphasize at the very outset that in this book we present an *introductory overview* of computer simulation modeling. Our intended audience is composed of readers who have an interest in simulation but as yet have not acquired the skills they need to make it an integral part of their analytic tool kit. We do not assume that our readers are experienced computer users, let alone proficient programmers. The basic ideas involved in simulation tend to be quite simple, so most of the material we present here should be accessible to readers with little or no relevant background. It is also true, however, that some specific aspects of simulation are complex, demanding considerable technical expertise. We would be gratified but amazed if readers of this book came away from it with the skills they need to conduct any but the most rudimentary computer simulation. Among other things, the fledgling modeler needs to acquire programming skills—skills we make no attempt to teach in this volume. Rather, our purpose is to try to instill in readers a certain analytical orientation, a cast of mind that opens up new ways of thinking about phenomena of interest, and to get our readers started on the road toward mastery of simulation methods and techniques.

COMPUTER SIMULATION AS THE INTERSECTION OF SIMULATION, MODELING, AND COMPUTER-FACILITATED RESEARCH

Computer simulation modeling represents the intersection of three distinct research tools or analytic approaches: system simulation, modeling, and the use of the digital computer as a research aid.

Types of Simulation

There are three primary types of simulation in social science. Person-person simulation involves interaction between two or more people in a laboratory environment representing some situation of interest. Much research on small-group decision making, for example, proceeds by bringing people together in a carefully controlled setting and observing their interaction patterns. Person-person simulations also are used in non-laboratory settings for heuristic or learning purposes. A common example is the mock job interview, designed to provide "simulated" experience in coping with interview questions before a job candidate participates in a real interview; in some mock interviews, the job candidate may also perform the role of the interviewer in order to gain further insight into the motives and perceptions of interviewers. Person-person simulations also are widely used for entertainment, as in the controversial game "Dungeons and Dragons." In this game, each player assumes the persona of a certain character and then simulates the behavior of that character, carried to its logical conclusion.

Person-machine simulation involves interaction between a computer program and a person responding to input from the computer, with the individual's responses influencing future input from the computer. Business strategy games that have been incorporated into many business school curricula are a common type of person-machine simulation. Such games are intended to enhance students' decision-making skills, especially under conditions defined by limited time and information. These games vary in focus from how to undertake a corporate takeover to how to expand a company's share of the market. Typically, the player feeds information into a computer program and receives back a series of options or additional data that are conditional upon the player's initial choices. The game proceeds through several series of these interactive, iterative steps.

By contrast, machine or all-computer simulations, which are the primary focus of this book, do not require player input while the simulation is executing. A machine simulation involves feeding input into a computer program, which then uses explicitly defined decision rules to transform input values into output values. For example, a program from physics emulates the "Big Bang" conception of the origin of the universe, simulating the growth and spatial dispersion of galaxies that would emerge if the universe had, indeed, begun with a "Big Bang."

Types of Models

Models take many forms. As we have already noted, a physical model purports to be a physical replica of the system being studied. A wind tunnel is a physical model that engineers build and use to simulate atmospheric conditions and air currents. The performance of scale models of proposed aircraft and automobiles is tested in the wind tunnel before the expense of building a life-size prototype for testing in "real" flying or driving conditions is incurred. A schematic model, on the other hand, includes diagrams, maps, and charts of the system. A flowchart, often developed prior to computer simulation, is a type of schematic model; a more common schematic model is the blueprint of a house, and an even more common one is a road map. A symbolic model is based on mathematics or computer code (Fishman, 1973). For example, etched into the brain of every introductory economics student is the equation $Y = C + I + G$, where Y refers to the Gross National Product, C is the dollar value of consumption, I is the dollar value of investment, and G is the dollar value of government spending.

Whatever form it may take, the model itself typically is a representation of a structure, while the simulation is a representation of the structure in action. In this sense, a road map is a model of a system of streets. Using the framework provided by the map, a transportation specialist might simulate traffic flows within a particular area. Strictly speaking, simulations, as representations of processes rather than of a configuration of elements, are dynamic, unfolding over time between certain starting and ending points. "Model" and "simulation" often are used interchangeably, since in practice the two often are so closely interconnected that it is impossible to say where the one ends and the other begins; we do not view this terminological matter as particularly crucial.

Besides being categorized in terms of form, models also can be classified according to function. A useful way of categorizing models functionally is to describe them as intuitive, analytical, or numerical (Poole and Szymankiewicz, 1977). Intuitive models are not fully articulated, but underlie most everyday decisions that are based on experience and require a quick consideration of alternatives. Analytical models are more appropriate when problems are less restricted by time, including those where mistakes are potentially expensive. The factors involved and their interrelationships must be fully specified, typically in mathematical terms.

Computer simulation is best equipped to address numerical models. It is most appropriate when the problem under consideration is one about which suitable information is unavailable or unusually complex, or both. In such circumstances, simulation allows one to conduct systematic theoretical experiments. Computer simulation requires the problem solver to identify the most important components of the process being simulated, to specify the most important forces operating on these components, and to describe the dynamic relationships among these components and forces. The greater one's understanding of the process being simulated, the more useful the results the simulation is likely to produce. Even when, as is sometimes the case, simulation proves laborious and expensive and fails to produce an acceptable (let alone an optimal) answer, it forces the researcher into better understanding of the process, or at least to a better understanding of what is not known about the process.

Uses of the Computer

Computer simulation by definition involves the use of a computer. First developed at the end of World War II, computers are used for two main purposes. The first is the rapid storage, updating, retrieval, and manipulation of information. Because of its tremendous speed and accuracy, the computer surpasses humans in dealing with large volumes of information. The computer is capable of rapidly "remembering" everything it has been told and of performing complex sorting and selective retrieval operations upon everything in its memory—capacities that not even the most retentive human could ever hope to match. An additional attraction is the compression of data into electromagnetic form for easy and efficient storage; it is now commonplace for a single microcomputer floppy disk to store upwards of a million characters of information, and emerging technologies will soon dwarf even that impressive capacity.

Analysis is the second major application of the computer. The computer can rapidly scan a large volume of information to look for specified patterns. It can conduct logical operations and arithmetic calculations at speeds and accuracies far surpassing those of the human brain. The rise of quantification in social science is closely tied to the advent of computers, and for good reason. Performing complex statistical operations on data sets of even modest size is a daunting task if one is doing it by hand. Computers, however, open up new possibilities for data analysis that were not previously available or practical.

In other words, the computer is, in some very important senses, a super abacus capable of making extraordinarily rapid calculations, and a wonderfully accurate and efficient recorder of information. These are important contributions, but simulation progresses far beyond using the computer as a recorder, storer, and manipulator of information. Simulation in effect places a laboratory within the computer, allowing the analyst to engage in experimentation that was not previously possible. The analyst is able to do this by entering an abstract world of symbols and computer code that represent real world phenomena. By manipulating the symbols under controlled conditions, the analyst can extrapolate what would happen to the real-world phenomena if these phenomena were manipulated directly instead of in a simulated fashion.

Simulations can be conducted on various types of computers, ranging from microcomputers to mainframes. Each type has certain advantages. Mainframes have enormous storage capacity and computing power, but for various reasons (e.g., poor access or great expense) they may be inconvenient or impossible to use. At the other extreme, microcomputers have more limited capacity and speed, but they have the offsetting advantages of convenient location (on one's desktop), economy, and ease of operation. Of course, simulation is not the only, or even the main use of digital computers in social science research. Indeed, statistical analysis far outweighs simulation as a social science computer application.

Computer Simulation as an Intersection

Computer simulation, then, operates at the intersection of modeling, simulation, and the computer. The basic structure for a computer simulation is provided by an abstract model representing the system under investigation, symbolically represented by programming language codes. The simulation may incorporate mathematics, but does not necessarily do so. Computer simulation is an all-machine form of simulation whose primary purpose is knowledge generation. This knowledge may aid the theorist in theory building or the practitioner in forecasting and planning. Computer simulation represents the use of a computer for analytic goals rather than for simply warehousing large amounts of data.

THE ELEMENTS OF COMPUTER SIMULATION

Five elements comprise a computer simulation: (1) assumptions upon which the simulation is built; (2) parameters, or fixed values; (3) inputs, or independent variables; (4) algorithms, or process decision rules; and (5) outputs, or dependent variables. Ideally, theoretical principles provide the underlying assumptions and algorithms. Computer simulations are similar to standard inductive research designs in that both employ independent, dependent, and control variables. They differ in that in simulations the dependent variable values are determined by the algorithms driving the simulation rather than by observation and measurement.

Of the large array of inductive research designs, it is experimental, rather than observational, quasi-experimental, or nonexperimental designs that most closely resemble computer simulation. In experimental designs, as in simulations, the researcher is able to control for extraneous or confounding events and to set and manipulate the initial values of the independent variables. In observational, quasi-experimental, and nonexperimental designs, the researcher rarely can manipulate the independent variables or hold constant the values of the control variables.

Assumptions

Assumptions underlie all computer simulations. In other types of research, the primary assumptions are the major research hypotheses, often expressed statistically as both a null hypothesis that no relationship exists between the independent and dependent variable, and an alternative hypothesis that there is a linkage between the independent and dependent variable.

Research hypotheses also are used in computer simulation. For example, a political scientist simulating the process by which a citizen decides which presidential candidate to vote for might hypothesize (just as would a political scientist examining data from an opinion survey) that, other factors remaining equal, the voter will select whichever candidate takes stands on the most salient issues that most nearly match the voter's own policy views. Simulation differs somewhat from observational and other types of empirical research, however, in that additional assumptions also are identified. These additional assumptions are substantive and reflect the particular nature of the phenomenon being modeled. Assumptions also serve as a guide for decision processes incorporated into the simulation, and must therefore be compatible with those decision processes. In a sense, assumptions form the skeletal structure of a simulation model. To extend the anatomical analogy, the energy-generating inputs of food and rest are analogous to the independent variables in a simulation, while the resulting energy-expending behaviors are analogous to the primary dependent variable.

Parameters

Parameters are similar to control variables in empirical research. Parameters could vary, but they are fixed at a particular value during the simulation exercise. Like control variables in an experiment, parameters are presumed to have some potential impact on variation in the dependent variable. They are held constant in order to minimize that impact, permitting the researcher to attribute variation in the dependent variable to the independent variables being tested. Just as in experimental research, where the ability to hold control variables constant clarifies the issue of causality, in simulation the ability to fix parameters at a constant level constitutes a vital analytic advantage.

Input Variables and Values

Independent variables in a computer simulation model are analogous to independent variables in experimental research. In each instance they are construed as factors that affect the primary phenomenon of interest, the dependent variable. In each case, too, independent variables are manipulated by the researcher. In experimental research, such manipulation is physical; for example, social psychologists interested in the impact of physical attractiveness on impression formation would show pictures of more and less attractive people to their experimental subjects and record the responses that the different pictures evoke. By contrast, in computer simulation the manipulation of the independent variable is symbolic. For example, in a simulation designed to test the impact of various speed limits upon auto accidents, the researcher may manipulate the independent variable by specifying, for simulation purposes, speed limits of 55, 65, and 75 miles per hour.

It follows that in computer simulation, the researcher must establish the range of values for each independent variable. This is the equivalent of a medical researcher, for example, deciding what dosages (independent variable values) or levels of a drug to administer to groups participating in an experiment.

Algorithms

Algorithms, or decision rules, form the muscles of a computer simulation. The actual work of the simulation is conducted by the algorithms, which convert inputs into outputs according to rules the researcher has specified. These algorithms must be compatible with the assumptions underlying the model, but they are more specific than the assumptions; in the language of research design, they are "operationalizations" of model structure and processes.

Output Variables and Values

The dependent variable is both the primary phenomenon of interest in a computer simulation and the main output of the simulation model. As in other types of research, the researcher identifies the dependent variables to be used in the simulation, guided by theoretical concerns and/or real world problems. The processes incorporated into the computer simulation model, in the form of the algorithms, then determine the value of the dependent variable under various combinations of independent variable values. The dependent variable values are thus determined endogenously (from within the model), while the independent variables are exogenously set by the researcher.

SOME USES OF COMPUTER SIMULATION

Once the structure of a computer simulation model has been developed, the model is ready to be used. A primary use of computer simulation is theory building. In theory building, computer simulation offers the researcher many of the advantages of a classical experimental design, but without many of the associated costs. A second use of computer simulation is policy planning, including prediction of the consequences of specific policies, as well as comparison of alternative policies to suggest which will produce more desirable outcomes.

Social scientists have used computer simulation to study such diverse problems as the dynamics of the turtle population on the Australian Great Barrier Reef and the impact of affirmative action policies on the composition of the work force. To convey a sense of how computer simulations work, let us consider two quite different simulation exercises.

A Simulation of International Conflict

Our first example is a simulation by Richard Stoll (1983), who was interested in the vital issue of why nations go to war against one another. This is a theoretical issue of the first order, though it also is obviously replete with policy implications. The purpose of the simulation was to predict the behavior of nations involved in serious disputes with one another. In the 160 years between 1816 and 1975, there were 225 occasions on which military force was threatened or actually used in disputes involving major powers, but only about 12% of these led to war. Stoll simulated the occurrence of serious international disputes with the intention of predicting how these disputes would turn out—most importantly, whether they would result in war.

Stoll began with the general notion that a conflict of interest between nations exists whenever their preferences cannot be satisfied simultaneously. Conflicts of interest exist between many nations at any point in time, but they do not become overtly conflictual unless governments are aware of the problem and engage in some sort of communication about it.

At the stage of overt conflict, nations have several options—ignoring the problem, giving in to the other side, trying to influence the other parties involved, seeking the aid of third parties, using diplomatic or economic alternatives, or threatening or actually using military force. Serious conflict occurs when military force is threatened or used.

According to Stoll, there are three levels of military conflict: threatening to use force, displaying force, and actually using it. Each level of conflict has various subtypes. The threat of force includes threatening to blockade, to declare war, to seize or occupy territory, or to use other types of military intervention. The display of force includes calling a military alert, mobilizing inactive military units, and demonstrating military presence without actual combat operations. The use of force includes blockading, firing at target forces or invading and seizing territory, and seizing personnel and materials.

Stoll employed a data set on serious disputes among major powers between 1816 and 1975. Guided by the variables in this data set, he wrote a simulation model in the FORTRAN IV language. (Computer languages and software are discussed in Chapter 4.) The purpose of the simulation was to predict a future action by a nation involved in a dispute. The nation whose actions were being predicted was called X, while the nation toward which X was directing its action was called Y.

The simulation model employed four groups of decision rules, arranged in two tiers. In the bottom tier were three sets of rules designed to simulate the diplomatic service (which scans the relationship between X and Y); the military service (which scans the military balance between X and Y); and the intelligence service (which scans the intelligence balance between X and Y). In the top tier were rules to simulate the central decision-making unit (CDU) of X. The CDU was defined as having no direct access to the environment, but rather as using the three lower level evaluations to generate predictions. The CDU could accept or reject information from the lower tier, but could not reevaluate or replace such information.

Stoll configured the model so that the diplomatic routine would scan data on past interactions between X and Y and assess hostility as a function of prior discord. It would offer recommendations to respond at either the current level of hostility, a lower level, or a higher level. If, for example, there had been a war between the nations during the past 25 years, the diplomatic routine would recommend escalation to one hostility level higher than the current incident. Thus if the precipitating incident were a display of force, the diplomatic routine would also recommend elevating the hostility level if there had been at least one serious dispute between the two nations during the previous 10 years. If there had been no war during the past 25 years but there had been a serious dispute during that period, the diplomatic routine would recommend responding at the same level of hostility as the precipitating incident. The absence of diplomatic relations between the two nations would cause this recommendation to be increased by one hostility level. Only if there were a formal military bond between the two nations would the recommended level of response be reduced by one hostility level from that of the precipitating incident.

The military routine was designed to examine the military balance (ratio of military expenditures) between X and Y at the time of the dispute, suitably modified by the geographic proximity of the dispute to the two nations. If the dispute were contiguous to the nation, its full military resources would be available. If the dispute were in the same geographic area but not contiguous, two thirds of the nation's military resources would be available. For nations with a significant naval capacity, one third of military expenditures would be available for disputes outside the region. For nations lacking a significant naval capacity, 1% of military resources would be available for disputes outside the region. After X and Y's resources were modified according to these rules, they were placed in a ratio of one to the other.

Next, the ratio was adjusted for the effect of previous wars. If X had lost a war within 25 years to some nation other than Y, 1 would be subtracted from the ratio, and if the lost war was to Y, 2 would be subtracted from the ratio. If Y had lost a war within 25 years but not to X, 1 would be added to the ratio, and if Y's loss had been to X, 2 would be added to the ratio.

As a last step in this part of the lower tier, the military capability ratio would be modified according to the level of action to be undertaken. If the final ratio were 1:3 or less (that is, if Y had a 3:1 military superiority over X), a recommendation for no action would be forwarded to the CDU. For ratios between 1:3 and 1:1, a recommendation for an action one level higher than that of the precipitating incident would be forwarded. For ratios greater than 1:1, where X would have a clear military advantage, the military routine would recommend a one-step increase in hostility. If the site of the dispute were contiguous, all recommendations for no action would be replaced by recommendations for threatening to use force.

Finally, the intelligence routine would estimate the long-term mobilization capacity of X and Y based on their resources (military personnel, military expenditures, steel production, commercial energy consumption, total population, and urban population). A total capacity ratio between X and Y would be calculated by averaging these six ratios for the two nations.

How, based on all these inputs, was the CDU to make decisions? If the recommendations of the diplomatic service and military command were for the same level of hostility, then the CDU used that level as its response. If the two recommendations differed, the recommendation from the intelligence command would be examined. If the total capacity ratio from the intelligence command was less than 1:1, the CDU would follow the less hostile of the recommendations from the diplomatic service and military command. If the total capacity ratio exceeded 1:1, the CDU would follow the more hostile of the two recommendations.

To test this model of nations "at the brink," Stoll used 11 incidents involving Japan and Russia between 1895 and 1903. One methodological problem was how to match incidents with responses, an issue Stoll dealt with by assuming that if X acted within 30 days of an incident perpetrated by Y, X was responding to Y; if not, no response had occurred. For the Japanese, only 3 of the 11 incidents and responses were predicted correctly, while for the Russians the model predicted correctly 5 times out of 11. So the model did not perform all that well, in the sense of its accuracy in reproducing the actual historical response. Even though the percentage of exact matches between predicted and actual responses was not all that impressive, there was, however, a strong correlation between how hostile an action or response was predicted to be and how hostile it actually was. So the model clearly pointed in the right direction, which was encouraging in light of the complexity of the decision process being modeled and the relative simplicity of the simulation model.

A Simulation of Contest Structures
and Outcomes

Have you ever watched a contest of some sort (perhaps the "Miss America" pageant, a boxing match, or a public speaking competition) and come away feeling that the best contestant did not win? This is a common occurrence—so common, in fact, that Warren Thorngate and Barbara Carroll (1987) suspected that there may be something embedded in the very structure of contests that tends to produce the "wrong" winner. In order to cast light on this question, Thorngate and Carroll designed and carried out a computer simulation of contests.

Contests can be conducted according to a host of alternative rules. One typical contest structure is to begin with local competitions, from which the local winners progress to regional contests, with winners then going on to provincial or semifinal rounds, and then to national competition. Yet errors can creep in along the way, because judges are fallible and because good contestants have off days and may be eliminated. Indeed, as contestants progress into higher rounds and compete with opponents of more similar ability, the probability increases that one or two minor errors may eliminate them.

Some contests have been constructed to try to reduce or minimize error. For example, in expert-rated contests, such as gymnastics or music competitions or dance contests, the scores from two or more judges are averaged at lower levels of competition, and the number of judges is increased at higher levels. Some contests average scores across several rounds to compensate for "bad days" by participants. Others require contestants to perform increasingly difficult skills as they progress to higher rounds. Some use double elimination to prevent premature elimination of qualified competitors due to one loss. Of course, no contest structure is guaranteed to be error-free, in the sense that it will invariably select as the winner the most deserving contestant. How error-free should a contest structure be in order to be acceptable? At the very least, Thorngate and Carroll contend, if N competitors participate, the probability that the best is selected should be greater than $1/N$; that is, the contest structure should outperform a random selection procedure in selecting the winner. Obviously, too, the closer the contest structure is to being 100% error-free, the better.

To determine the relationship between various contest structures and the chances that the best candidate will win, Thorngate and Carroll ran several thousand simulations of contests. The simulated contests varied in the following aspects: (1) the number of contestants participating in the first round of competition; (2) the number of elimination rounds; (3) the amount of random judgment error involved in rating each contestant's performances; and (4) the extent of "seeding" of good contestants in early preliminary rounds. The point of the simulation was to see how changes in each of these variables would affect the probability that the best contestant in each contest would emerge as the winner.

Each contest in the various simulations began with the assignment of a true talent score (TTS) to each simulated contestant. To form each contestant's TTS, two random numbers were drawn from a uniform distribution that ranged from 0 to 50 (i.e., a distribution in which 0, 1, 2, . . . 50 all appeared an equal number of times). The TTS for any simulated contestant was then formed by adding these two numbers, so that the TTS could fall anywhere between 0 and 100. The result of adding these two randomly selected numbers from a uniform distribution was a triangular distribution (similar to a normal distribution) in which very few participants (2.9%) had scores above 90 and very few (2.9%) had scores below 10. Most participants (67%) had a TTS score within 20 points one way or the other of the mean (50).

Every time a contestant "performed," the resulting performance score (PS) was calculated by adding a random error term to the TTS of the contestant. This reflected the basic idea that contestants would perform largely according to form, but that their performance would vary a bit from one round to the next, as would the accuracy of the judging. The random error factor was calculated by drawing a random number from another triangular distribution. The range of errors was varied across the simulations, being increased by five, with each successive set of simulation runs. In one set, errors ranged from -2.5 to $+2.5$; in a second set, from -5.0 to $+5.0$; in a third set, from -7.5 to $+7.5$; and so on, up through -15.0 to $+15.0$. The computer program was written in both the BASIC and FORTH programming languages.

In an initial set of "control" or "baseline" computer runs the contest involved no hierarchy. Subsequent sets of runs tested the impact of different contest rules. For each run, the number of contestants was fixed at either 10, 100, or 1000. Each contestant was assigned a TTS and then "performed" once and obtained a PS through the combination of random error to the TTS, as described in the last paragraph. The contestant with the highest PS was declared the winner. A check was then performed to see whether the winner was the contestant with the highest TTS. The contest was repeated 1,000 times for each error range and each number of contestants. In all, 18,000 contests in total were examined, with new true talent scores and performance scores generated for contestants in each. The number of contests in which the winner had the highest TTS score was counted (18). These were interpreted as probability estimates that the best person would win. Other simulation runs varied other elements of the contest.

From these simulations, Thorngate and Carroll reached three general conclusions: (1) as the number of contestants increases, luck (i.e., random errors for the better or the worse by contestants and/or by judges) becomes more important in determining the contest winner; (2) the structure of the contest—whether it is hierarchical, winner-challenger, seeded, or free-for-all—has no noticeable effect on the overall chances that the best contestant will win, but in hierarchical elimination contests, the role played by luck does increase in later elimination rounds; (3) methods such as averaging individual performance scores over rounds in hierarchical contests can reduce but not eliminate the effects of luck. It follows that contests, no matter how they are configured, will inevitably involve an element—and sometimes a very large element—of sheer luck, but also that those organizing contests can take some fairly simple steps to minimize the luck element and increase the chances of rewarding the most deserving contestants.

To help make our earlier discussion of the five elements of computer simulation models more concrete, let us pause to record the components of the Stoll and Thorngate-Carroll simulations.

(1) Assumptions

Stoll

A response to a precipitating event must occur within 30 days.

Nations respond to each other in a manner positively correlated with the severity of the incident.

Responses can be matched with only one precipitating event (i.e., there is a one-to-one mapping between precipitating incidents and responses).

Thorngate and Carroll

Contestants' performance scores equal their basic talent score combined with an error term.

(2) Parameters

Stoll

A dispute between nations X and Y will not be affected by the intervention of other nations; that is, all disputes are dyadic.

Thorngate and Carroll

The distribution of talent in any given contest is "triangular" (quasi-normal).

(3) **Input Variables and Values**

Stoll

The severity of the precipitating incident;

The proximity of the conflict to the nation;

The data needed to calculate the military and total capacity ratios.

Thorngate and Carroll

The number of contestants;

The structure of the contest;

The range of error to be combined with a contestant's TTS score.

(4) **Algorithms**

Stoll

The three routines for the diplomatic service, military command, and intelligence service, and the routine for the Central Decision Making Unit

Thorngate and Carroll

Rules for generating a triangular distribution of TTS scores;

Rules for generating the distribution of errors;

A rule for combining the TTS scores and the errors;

A rule for selecting the "winner" of the contest.

(5) **Output Variables and Values**

Stoll

Whether or not a response from X occurred after the precipitating incident initiated by Y;

The severity of X's response.

Thorngate and Carroll

Comparison of the contest winner to the highest TTS score to determine whether the winner had the highest TTS score;

The percentage of contests in which the winner had the highest TTS score.

THE UTILITY OF COMPUTER SIMULATION MODELS

Even on the basis of examining only two computer simulation modeling exercises, it should be apparent that social scientists can simulate an *extremely diverse array of phenomena*. These phenomena range from psychological processes that occur within a single human being to social, political, and economic processes that characterize an entire nation. This flexibility constitutes a distinct advantage of computer simulation modeling over alternative modes of analysis. Any system that can be represented by symbolic terms and logical processes can be simulated.

It also should be obvious that simulation can assume a *diversity of forms*. A simulation may be developed as a means of presenting a formal theory with no recourse to empirical data (as in the contest simulation), as a means of presenting a formalized account of empirical data (as in the international conflict simulation), or as some combination of the two. The fact that there are multiple ways simulations can be developed and conducted underlines the flexibility of this method as an analytic tool.

Even though they are relatively simple, the two simulations outlined above also make it clear that a simulation model can provide a framework for the analysis of a *large array of variables*. A great deal can go on simultaneously or serially in a simulation—far more than any individual can keep organized in his or her mind. This ability to trace the operation of numerous variables simultaneously facilitates theory formation while permitting the specification of sufficient detail so that the match between model and reality remains acceptably close.

Computer simulation also provides *extraordinary efficiency* by permitting the researcher to manipulate the major components of a complex system without actually constructing or physically replicating the system itself. In this way, the cost, inconvenience, and time involved in experimentation on the actual system or on small-scale versions of it can be avoided.

Computer simulation *expands the ability of researchers to analyze problems for which empirical data are unavailable*. Due to political or ethical considerations or to the irreversible nature of the change process in the real world, actual experimentation in many cases not only is costly, but impossible, leaving computer models as the only practical means of bringing disciplined analysis to bear on theoretical or policy issues.

Additionally, computer simulation is *dynamic in nature*. Computer simulation incorporates an explicit time dimension. Dynamic models have two major advantage s over static models. They are more realistic, since time influences real-world systems. Moreover, unlike most static models, they avoid the shortcomings of equilibrium assumptions. The equilibrium assumption often fails to describe, explain, and predict social phenomena, because many real-world systems evolve incrementally rather than strive toward equilibrium. On the other hand, dynamic models have some problems of their own. For example, observations in a given series may display autocorrelation, which occurs, in the simplest case, when the value of an observation at time t is a function of the value at time $t - 1$. Such temporal autocorrelation undermines the researcher's ability to probe relations across variables. Dynamic models also can produce biased simulation output caused by the impact of the initial conditions on system behavior, compounded across time (Apter, 1970).

Some simulation models feature *stochastic disturbances* (random error). The contest simulation, for example, builds random error directly into the simulation by using it to represent fluctuations in performance by contestants and judges. Using a random number generator to either distribute input variables or to determine the outcome of decision rules introduces stochastic variation into the simulation results. Variability in the output data is introduced by the inclusion of stochastic elements in the simulation model, causing the numerical results of a particular run to become an element in a broader sample of outcomes.

Introducing output variance through the inclusion of stochastic elements has both advantages and disadvantages. A disadvantage is that the researcher cannot always produce exactly the same results via replication (as would occur, for example, in the international conflict simulation, which does not involve any stochastic disturbances). The researcher must undertake a number of replications and discuss the results in terms of statistical probabilities. An advantage of including stochastic variation is that such variation more closely resembles random forces in the real world. It can be used to simulate nonrandom but unknown forces as well, through the inclusion of different types of statistical distributions.

A PREVIEW OF COMING ATTRACTIONS

In this chapter we have introduced some basic ideas underlying computer simulation in the social sciences and we have glimpsed some illustrative applications of computer simulation. Having done so, we are in position to consider the advantages and disadvantages computer simulation holds out for users and the strategies and techniques that are involved in computer simulation.

In Chapter 2 we begin by highlighting the distinction between deductive and inductive reasoning, and use that distinction as a bridge to a discussion of the assumptions underlying computer simulation modeling. Computer simulation, we argue, is a valuable tool for both policy planning and analysis.

In Chapter 3 we take a closer look at computer simulation, in terms of the specific steps that are involved in a simulation and the concrete choices that the modeler must make in building a simulation model—choices about what type of simulation to employ, how to handle the time dimension, how to generate random numbers and variates, how to design the simulation "experiment," and how to address questions of causality.

In Chapter 4, the discussion becomes more technical still, probing issues related to programming languages, model validation, statistical analysis, and defending against errors of various sorts.

In Chapters 5, 6, and 7, we present three concrete examples of simulation models, in order to demonstrate for the novice how general theoretical or policy ideas are translated into a simulation model, what considerations go into a model, how a model actually operates, and so forth. The first sample simulation is in a theoretical vein and the second in a policy analysis vein. Both of these are examples of deterministic models and, therefore, the third simulation exemplifies a stochastic model.

Chapter 8 brings our introductory overview of computer simulation modeling to a close by summarizing and reflecting upon the material presented.

Readers who are generally unfamiliar with computer simulation modeling will not come away from this book as skilled professional modelers. In order to actually undertake computer simulations, novices will have to acquire skills, such as computer programming, that we make no attempt to teach here. This process should be facilitated by the introductory overview, and by the bibliography of more advanced materials provided at the end of this book. If we are successful, readers will acquire a good general sense of what computer simulation modeling is about and what its potential might be in their own work.

2

A Model for All Seasons: Simulation in Theory Building and Policy Analysis

In this chapter we show where simulation fits within the realm of scientific activity; discuss some assumptions underlying all computer simulation models; and, most importantly, examine the strengths and weaknesses of simulation as a tool for theory building and policy planning.

TWO TYPES OF REASONING: DEDUCTION AND INDUCTION

Simulation can be and usually is both inductive and deductive. Characteristic of the deductiveness of simulation is the need to make assumptions from which various consequences logically follow. Characteristic of the inductiveness of simulation is the derivation of algorithms from empirical observation of the real-world system. Some simulations of voting behavior, for example, use algorithms based on majority rule, a principle observed in many political systems. Although as citizens of democratic systems we often take this principle for granted, it should be obvious that different empirically derived algorithms could be used as a basis for simulating voting behavior.

Deductive or axiomatic reasoning requires a premise, a conclusion, and a justification linking the two. In deductive reasoning, if the premises are true, then the conclusion is necessarily true. Deductive reasoning, which is often mathematical in form, is guided by sets of axioms.

A deductive axiomatic system should exhibit both consistency and independence. The consistency criterion implies that it is impossible to prove both a theorem and its negation. For example, in economic theory a competitive market cannot be moving toward equilibrium and away from it at the same time. Independence implies that no basic axiom can be proved by knowing only the remaining axioms. If an axiom is entirely knowable on the basis of other axioms, then it really contributes nothing. Thus, for example, in Euclidean geometry the basic axiom that a straight line is the shortest distance between two points could not be proved by knowing that parallel lines never meet if extended into space, or by knowing any other axioms or any other set of axioms. Axiomatic systems may also exhibit completeness, but do not always do so. If every statement concerning the basic terms can either be proved or disproved within the axiomatic system, the system is said to be complete. Darwin's theory of evolution at the time was incomplete, in the sense that one proposition assumed the existence of some type of inherited characteristics that were randomly distributed among the next generation. At the time, Mendel and others had not yet proved the existence of genes, nor could the existence of such entities be proven within the basic two-axiom system, in which the second axiom asserted that those species that survived had the characteristics that best matched environmental conditions.

In contrast to the deterministic nature of deductive reasoning, an *inductive* argument is accepted when the truth of its premises establishes an appropriately high probability that the conclusions are true. Thus inductive arguments do not always convey "truth," because a proper inductive argument may lead to an empirically false conclusion even though all the premises in the argument are true. Otherwise inductive arguments would be deductive (Giere, 1988; Kaplan, 1964). As a simple example of an inductive argument leading to an empirically false conclusion, consider the inductively derived generalization that women, in general, possess less physical strength than men. Applying this inductive generalization in any particular comparison of a specific man and a specific woman may well lead to an incorrect conclusion.

Science involves building and testing theories—sets of consistent, coherent propositions or theorems about a phenomenon of interest. The foremost use of deductive reasoning in scientific work is in developing new propositions through the manipulation of an axiomatic system. Since the axioms may well be stated in mathematical format, manipulating them in mathematically acceptable ways may produce new perspectives on the phenomena in question—perspectives that would not have been readily apparent in the absence of such manipulation. Game theory, for example, is the result of concerted efforts to build a theory of collective choice through manipulation of an axiomatic system based predominantly on set theory mathematics. The logic of the deductive axiomatic system produces theorems that become propositions in the theory. Deduction as a reasoning process facilitates theory building.

a theory-testing orientation has accompanied the deductive process so that the axioms and justifications in the system have counterparts in the real world, then the theorems derived via deductive reasoning are more likely to be useful in building predictive theory; the danger of isolating the system from empirical referents is that the system can become a "world" unto itself, not tied to the phenomena of the real world. The predominant tools of theory building, an activity relying heavily on deductive reasoning, are mathematization and simulation.

Ideally, each proposition should embody a testable hypothesis stating a relationship between two or more theoretical constructs. Through measurement, each construct is operationalized into a variable. The hypothesis (e.g., "The greater the X, the greater the Y") may be directional or nondirectional. A nondirectional hypothesis would simply state that X is different from, or not equal to Y. A directional hypothesis would be that X is greater than Y or, alternatively, that X is less than Y. Hypotheses also may be correlational, stating merely that two concepts covary, or causal, stating that variation in one concept depends on variation in the other. While statistical analysis facilitates the testing of both correlational and causal hypotheses, statistical analysis alone cannot deal conclusively with the issue of causality. Only experimental designs—which make use of a control group, random assignment of subjects to groups, and experimenter manipulation of the independent or "treatment" variables—possess the internal validity required for testing causal hypotheses (Cook and Campbell, 1979).

Inductive reasoning, including probabilistic and statistical reasoning, is critical to theory testing. Inductive reasoning involves replicative studies and tests to establish the long-run probabilities of a certain outcome (the dependent variable or conclusion of the inductive argument), given certain conditions (the independent variables or premises of the inductive argument). For example, in psychology hundreds of studies have been conducted to test the impact of frustration on aggression. No single study is definitive, but patterns that emerge over the course of many studies provide a firmer basis for generalizations about the link between frustration and aggression.

As a predominantly inductive task, theory testing is less reliant upon computer simulation than upon statistical analysis of empirical data. Some simulations do employ empirical data to demonstrate their validity but, in general, computer simulation remains a more powerful tool for theory building than for theory testing. Nor is computer simulation of much use in communicating theories and their implications to other scientific fields or to the public—a critical phase of scientific research in which purely verbal presentation and description predominate.

Simulation is useful, however, in assessing the policy implications of scientific theories. The social scientist Kurt Lewin (1975) was fond of saying that "There is nothing as practical as a good theory," and the well-trained practitioner or applied social scientist seizes upon theory for policy-planning purposes. Computer simulation provides a useful means of analyzing the outcomes of alternative policies when they are still under consideration and of forecasting or projecting the specific impacts of a particular policy. For example, when various changes in taxing and spending policy are being debated, simulations of the impacts on the economy as a whole, or of their effects on interest rates, government revenues, the federal deficit, and the inflation and unemployment rates often are undertaken. Similarly, simulations can help clarify the likely impact of proposed welfare programs on work incentives and employment. Of course, the simulations may or may not, depending upon one's point of view, produce credible results. At the very least, though, they force the contending parties to lay out explicitly the assumptions underlying the consequences they project. And, in situations where it is impossible to undertake an experiment or launch a pilot program, simulations may be the best one can do before the program is actually under way. Sensitivity testing (varying input conditions and observing the corresponding change in output values) with empirically derived models also is used for this purpose.

Along the same lines, Colella, O'Sullivan, and Carlino (1974) argue that the essential function of simulation is prediction. This may seem too narrow an interpretation, but they understand prediction in three different senses: (1) *prediction for evaluation* consists of ascertaining the performance of a proposed or existing system, including establishing the feasibility of system design; (2) *prediction for comparison* involves establishing the relationship between the performances of two different systems; and (3) *prediction for optimization* enables the forecaster to draw conclusions about which system is "best" in some sense. Of these three, prediction for evaluation and comparison are significant activities in theory building, while prediction for optimization is the essence of policy planning.

Colella et al. (1974) offer six criteria for determining the applicability of computer simulation to a particular situation. We consider it noteworthy that underlying these criteria is the recognition that simulations are a combination of deductive and inductive elements and that they are most applicable when based on real-world observation (induction). Computer simulation, as they see it, is a reasonable approach if

(1) it is impractical to experiment with the actual system in its natural environment;

(2) simulation provides the only means of investigating the design characteristics of a particular system (i.e., of permitting the researcher to "decompose" the system);

(3) analytic or mathematical techniques do not exist for the problem at hand, as is often the case with systems that incorporate substantial nonlinearities and irregularities;

(4) the complexity of the system precludes a tractable mathematical formulation and solution;

(5) the researcher is especially interested in generating sensitivity information in order to gain a basic understanding of the system and subsystem behavioral characteristics; and

(6) the system's performance must be assessed using statistical measures.

This is not, of course, to say that computer simulation must always be used *in preference to* another method, or even that the inductive element should dominate. One could, for example, use computer simulation to "formalize" a theoretical perspective on a given problem, specifying the components of the phenomenon and the linkages among them, and then go on to design a program of laboratory research to probe empirically the predictions generated by the model. Indeed, such multimethod approaches hold out great promise for theory building and testing, though, unfortunately, most problems still tend to be studied from a single methodological approach.

GENERIC ASSUMPTIONS OF SIMULATION

Any computer simulation is based on certain assumptions about the real-world system being modeled. Beyond these sorts of assumptions, however, simulation as a tool is based on certain methodological assumptions that do not depend upon the substance of the model (Elzas, 1984). Four of these generic assumptions are especially important:

(1) *Adequate system description.* The first of these methodological assumptions is that the system in question can be adequately described by a finite set of symbols and relations between and among these

symbols. What constitutes adequacy? Obviously, not every aspect of a system will be symbolically represented, or the model will become every bit as complex as the system it represents. In that case, the model would lose its appeal as an analytic tool, since its utility is based on its ability to present a simplified version or reduced form of the underlying system. So a one-to-one correspondence is not necessary and, often, it is not even desirable. Even so, whatever is omitted is presumed to be relatively incidental to the system's basic structure and operation. That is, the symbols and relations representing the system must capture the essential features of the system.

(2) *Explicit rules for symbol manipulation.* It is possible to simulate any system if it consists of a finite set of determinate elements related to each other by explicit rules. To be sure, the system can contain random elements, like the contest structure modeled by Thorngate and Carroll (1987) described in Chapter 1. But the operation of even the random elements must be explicitly spelled out in the rules describing the system.

(3) *Control of extraneous factors.* The system's environment is assumed either to be invariant or to change according to identifiable, determinate rules. For example, in Stoll's (1983) simulation of dyadic conflict in the international system (explained in Chapter 1), the influence of other nations was understood to be a fixed factor. It would have been possible for Stoll to construct a more complex model that took account of the influence of other nations upon the actions of the focal nations X and Y. Had he done so, he would, as provided by the second assumption, have had to incorporate into the simulation explicit rules covering such influence relations.

(4) *Correspondence to real-world systems.* Finally, the symbols developed and used must be intelligible and must convey a satisfactory level of knowledge about the system under study. This, in a sense, brings us back to the first assumption. For a simulation of, say, dyadic international conflict to be analytically useful, the simulation must pose a picture of conflict that is recognizable, at least in rough outline. If it is not, then the simulation might constitute at best a stimulating diversion with no particular utility for the analysis or prediction of events in the real world.

It is worth noting, however, that models differ greatly in the degree to which they map reality. A *calibrated* model is one whose parameters have been fitted or "tuned" to observational data obtained from the real system. Because calibration involves only parameters or control variables, it does not affect the degree of realism obtained by either model assumptions or algorithms. Nor does it test the appropriateness of model behavior. On the other hand, a *validated* model is one for which model-generated data have been compared to data generated by the real system (i.e., real and simulated dependent variable values) in order to ascertain the degree of behavioral similarity between the model and the system; Stoll (1983) did exactly this in his simulation of international conflict. Finally, a *realistic* model is a step beyond a validated model, in that not only the values of the model's outcome variables but also its structure and internal interactions have been validated. This involves gathering information about the real system relevant to model assumptions, algorithms, and parameters, and then comparing such information to model assumptions, algorithms, and parameter values in order to determine how realistic an understanding of the system the model conveys. The greater the isomorphism (that is, the greater the similarity between the model and the real system being modeled), the more realistic the model is said to be.

In social science, attempts to demonstrate the reality of a model typically involve, at most, calibration and validation, and even then validation is normally performed with only a single, limited set of empirical data. Rarely do social scientists possess sufficient data to demonstrate isomorphism between the model and the real system; nor do they often test predicted versus actual outcomes more extensively, across several sets of empirical data. Indeed, in many circumstances, as when one is trying to project the results of policies that have not yet been initiated or when one faces other obstacles to data collection, even a limited test of empirical versus predicted outcomes is not possible.

COMPUTER SIMULATION AS A
THEORY-BUILDING TOOL

Researchers using computer simulation as a theory building tool must be familiar with both the substantive area in which the theory is to be constructed and the technique of simulation. Current knowledge and theory are used to construct a model that ultimately will expand the theoretical base. In this regard, simulation modeling is similar to experimental research, in the sense that an experimental design incorporating current theory generates empirical findings that facilitate the expansion of theory. In computer simulation, however, the design of the computer model replaces the design of the experiment.

**Some Advantages of Computer Simulation
in Theory Building**

Computer simulation has numerous advantages as a tool for building
theory:

(1) *Flexibility*. Computer simulation provides greater flexibility in
constructing theory than do purely mathematical or statistical tools.
Other than the four generic assumptions of the technique, the limiting
assumptions in computer simulation are substantively specific; the
technique itself does not constrain the substantive assumptions the
modeler can make. Thus, for example, a model of recidivism in prisons
will make assumptions about the behavior of prisoners and their interactions with the environment, while a model of the economy will make
assumptions about the behavior of firms and workers in the economy.
The substantively specific assumptions in these two models will not
necessarily be equivalent, or even focused on the same issues. Those
relating to prisoners are likely to deal with propensities to commit
illegal acts, while those about firms and workers are likely to deal with
strategies to increase income. By contrast, mathematical tools such as
linear programming and statistical tools such as regression analysis
often require limiting assumptions that are not specific to the subject
being studied and which may, in any given inquiry, be substantively
inappropriate.

(2) *Ability to incorporate uncertainty*. The phenomena social scientists study encompass uncertainty, since no human act is *perfectly*
predictable. In traditional experimental and observational designs, uncertainties often are ignored. Or, if they are not ignored, they are
incorporated into the model only in the form of a random error term
assumed to be unconnected to any substantive component of the model.
In computer simulation, it is relatively easy to build uncertainties
directly into the algorithms or decision rules.

If the researcher wishes to retain stochastic variation in the model, a
random number generator may be employed. Or the researcher may
eliminate stochastic variation altogether by converting those quantities
about which the shape of variation is unknown into independent variables. In the latter case, the independent variables can be permitted to
vary systematically in sensitivity testing, so that the researcher does not
assume a distribution for the variable but rather examines the consequences if different levels of the variable were to occur.

(3) *Consideration of all possible combinations of independent variables*. In the real world, certain combinations of independent variable

levels are more likely than other combinations. Often, interesting hypothetical combinations are precluded from scrutiny, because they are not currently in existence or are very rare. Or, when they are in evidence, other variables may not be controlled, confounding any conclusions that could be drawn about the impact of the independent variable of interest. Computer simulation provides a way to circumvent this difficult problem in the analysis of social phenomena. Through computer simulation, all possible combinations of independent variables, or certain subsets of all possible combinations of interest, may be explored.

(4) *Examination of interaction effects.* A further advantage of examining the impacts of many or all combinations of independent variable levels through computer simulation is that doing so allows for more accurate tests of the interactive effects of these variables. When only one set or a limited set of independent variable values is examined, the full range of interactions cannot be explored. For example, a researcher interested in juvenile delinquency may posit a complex interaction whereby affluent youngsters of one racial group behave in a certain way, while less affluent youngsters of the same racial group and all youngsters (affluent or not) of a different racial group behave in a different way. In a given setting, however, there may be too few youngsters of a particular racial group and economic status to pursue this interactive interpretation. In such a situation, a simulation-based approach may present the researcher with some analytic alternatives that would not otherwise be available.

(5) *Dynamism.* Although most significant questions about social phenomena involve an explicit or implicit time dimension, many—perhaps most—observational studies are cross-sectional, reflecting the constraints of limited resources and the difficulty of tracking subjects or other phenomena over time. Even in experimental research, rarely do more than two points in time come into play—a preexperimental observation on the dependent variable and a posttest observation on the same variable. By contrast, computer simulation allows for dynamic tests of the impact of independent variables on the dependent variables. This dynamic potential is critical in identifying time-related curvilinear relationships and threshold levels.

Some Disadvantages of Computer Simulation in Theory Building

We consider computer simulation a powerful aid in theory building. It is not, however, without limitations. Since our purpose in this book is to help equip the reader to understand and use computer simulation as an analytic tool, we consider it vital to convey a sense of the limitations and shortcomings of computer simulation as well as its strong suits. In particular, computer simulation has several disadvantages as a theory building tool:

(1) *Omission of detail.* The abstractness of a computer model produces clarity, precision, and unambiguity. But abstraction also can constitute an Achilles' heel. Because a computer simulation presents an abstract model of some social process, many characteristics of the underlying process, including some that may be quite salient, are likely to be sacrificed, either inadvertently or purposefully. As a consequence, the simulation cannot be taken as an entirely faithful depiction of reality. Rather, it must be understood as reality abstracted and shorn of many of its defining "details." For example, even a reasonably complex simulation of the transmission of AIDS like the one we describe in Chapter 6 cannot possibly incorporate all the detail and complexity of AIDS transmission in the real world. Simulation models are simplifications, and have to be recognized as such. One who is not prepared to sacrifice some of the details and idiosyncracies that are found in the real world (the so-called "trees") for the sake of perceiving the broader picture (the so-called "forest") is ill-equipped to engage in computer simulation.

This, of course, is not a problem unique to computer simulation, as debates have raged for years in the social sciences about the relative merits of a broad understanding of phenomena that is not tied to specific places, people, or events, and deep understanding of phenomena that draws on the particularities of given cases.

(2) *Neophyte difficulty.* Another problem is the difficulty beginners may encounter in creating or understanding a simulation that operates at an appropriate level of sophistication or subtlety. One temptation is to oversimplify—to build a model so simple or naive that it is difficult even to imagine a real-world referent. The opposite temptation comes when the analysts try to account in the simulation for all the complexity they observe in the real-world system—to build a model so complex that it overtaxes their capacity or fails to clarify the system whose operation they are trying to simulate. Because computer simulation is flexible and relatively unstructured, it leaves open the possibility of erring in either direction and thereby accomplishing little. Only when the analyst possesses both technical facility in simulation and genuine familiarity with the subject matter is computer simulation likely to bear fruit.

(3) *Difficulty of model verification.* A third problem with computer simulation is the difficulty of verifying a model. Ideally, the researcher could verify every component of the structure of a simulation model, yet in practice this rarely occurs. Indeed, were empirical data as readily available as the verificationist perspective assumes, the rationale for simulation would be considerably weakened, as it would be possible to approach the research question via the more standard route of empirical data analysis.

Even if relevant data were available, it is unlikely that verification would be a straightforward exercise. For example, showing that one set of independent variable values in the model accurately predicts the dependent variable values does not verify the model. Because most models are complex and dynamic, a good fit between predicted and actual output for one set of input values does not necessarily mean that a similarly good fit will hold across other sets of input values. Even so, empirical validation is a necessary step if the insights generated through the use of a simulation model are to be incorporated eventually into a scientifically validated body of knowledge.

COMPUTER SIMULATION AS A
POLICY-PLANNING AND ANALYSIS TOOL

The second major use of computer simulation by social scientists is for policy planning and analysis. Informed policy planning presupposes an ability to anticipate the outcomes of policies whose adoption is under consideration. This is all the more pressing when resources are scarce. After a policy has been adopted, assessment of its impact means that one must be able to compare what actually happened after enactment to what would have happened in the absence of the policy. In either case—before or after a policy has been adopted—simulation constitutes a powerful tool for policy planning and analysis. For example, policy-makers could use a model of the sexual transmission of AIDS like the one described in Chapter 6 to try to anticipate whether particular programs might be effective and represent money well spent.

Some Advantages of Computer Simulation
in Policy Planning and Analysis

When designed to facilitate policy planning or analysis, computer simulation offers several advantages. Some of these, of course, are the same as in theory building. Beyond these commonalities, though, computer simulation presents policy analysts with several special advantages, such as the following:

(1) *Anticipation of specific policy outcomes.* Computer simulation in policy planning can provide reasonably concrete and specific information about the consequences of a particular policy before the policy is adopted or implemented. By definition, there can be no empirical data on the consequences of a policy before the policy has been adopted. Of course, the policy may have been implemented elsewhere but, even if it has, the applicability of empirical data drawn from other settings will be uncertain to the extent that the other settings differ from the one in which the policy is being considered. If, for example, the United States were seriously considering the development of a national health care system, proponents and opponents would doubtless use the British experience with national health care to try to assess the likely consequences of such a system. Limiting the applicability of the British experience, however, would be differences between the two nations in health problems, educational systems, and interest group configurations (to cite only three obvious points of divergence). When empirical data from elsewhere are of questionable applicability, a simulation model can provide a useful way of approaching the problem. Thus computer simulation can fulfill the need for reckoning with policy consequences in a novel setting. The larger the stakes, the more important it becomes to ponder the policy's possible consequences with the aid of available analytic tools such as simulation.

(2) *Testing alternative policies.* Computer simulation allows policy planners to test alternative policies (in the form of different independent variable values) under controlled circumstances in order to home in on the most appropriate or desirable policy. Hence computer simulation becomes a tool for facilitating informed decision making. Unlike the human mind, which can focus on only a limited number of the dimensions that need to be compared in policymaking, computer simulation makes it possible to include many dimensions, each appropriately weighted to approximate preference intensities, and to systematically factor these dimensions into the decision-making process. For example, if policymakers are considering various proposals for a tax cut, questions may arise about the likely economic impact of a tax cut. Working with a complex model of the national economy, policy analysts could simulate various types of tax cuts (say, cuts in personal or corporate income taxes), thereby providing a more reliable information base than

would otherwise be available to the policymakers who must support or oppose various proposals.

(3) *Testing different levels of policy implementation.* Computer simulation also allows for sensitivity testing to shed light on whether some levels of policy implementation as well as some policies are apt to be more effective than others. Sensitivity testing involves systematically varying input values in order to observe corresponding changes in output values. Such testing reflects the possibility that policies may fail not necessarily because the "wrong" policy has been chosen, but rather because the "right" policy is being administered at the "wrong" level. Sensitivity testing permits tests to be undertaken of alternative policies and of various levels of a given policy (such as, for example, small, moderate, or large cuts in personal income taxes).

(4) *Testing for unacceptable outcomes.* As an extension of sensitivity testing, computer simulation permits one to push independent variables to extreme values in order to gain a perspective on the point at which policies generate undesirable outcomes. In the real world, implementing policies with potentially dangerous outcomes in order to see when the dangerous outcomes occur makes no sense for an official whose primary concern is protecting the health and welfare of employees and clients; one cannot create a potential disaster simply to see whether the disaster will actually occur and what its effects will turn out to be. Such tests, however, can be conducted without harmful consequences in the context of a computer simulation model, and can provide useful information to policy planners concerning when danger zones are being approached. So computer simulation allows the testing of "worst case" scenarios in the abstract in order to avoid them in reality.

(5) *Examining tradeoffs.* Computer simulation enables one to explore, before a policy actually has been enacted, any likely tradeoffs between desirable outcomes of a particular policy that may occur across levels of implementation. For example, by systematically varying the level of foreign investment in a simulation model of the national economy, one could observe shifts in the tradeoff between short-term economic growth and dependency on foreign capital.

(6) *Low-cost planning.* Compared to other forms of analysis and to decision making with poor information, computer simulation is relatively inexpensive and efficient. The costs of implementing inappropriate policies, on the other hand, can be enormous. Field tests of social policies also are costly, and even when they are not financially prohibitive they are rarely feasible. By providing relatively quick and

inexpensive information prior to the implementation stage, computer simulation can mitigate some of these costs.

**Some Disadvantages of Computer Simulation
in Policy Planning and Analysis**

As is true of the advantages of computer simulation, there are many common *disadvantages* of computer simulation between theory building and policy planning and analysis. Some of these problems, however, are exacerbated in the policy context, as follows:

(1) *Difficulty in communicating the meaning, significance, and limitations of simulation-based findings.* In theoretical work, the primary audience for conclusions based on computer simulation is academic and scholarly. This audience is relatively well equipped to deal with both the forest and the trees of computer simulation. However, the audience for computer simulation-based policy analyses is more diverse. It includes legislators, administrators, and the general public as well as academicians. Conveying the nuances of computer simulations of possible policy outcomes to such a diverse audience is extremely challenging. Sometimes presentations bog down in trivial detail, but at other times they are so bereft of detail that even the most determined and sophisticated reader must accept on the basis of faith alone the conclusions based on the simulation.

(2) *Difficulties in verification.* As noted above, verification of computer-simulation-generated findings is difficult. If a policy considered desirable on the basis of simulation results is actually implemented, comparing the policy's predicted and actual outcomes requires unambiguous measurement of policy outcomes on the same scale employed in the computer simulation. Verification is further hamstrung by the understandable tendency of policymakers to choose only one policy at a time from among the possible alternatives. A single data point or case is sufficient neither to verify nor to diversify a model.

(3) *The requirement for technical sophistication.* Even in an era marked by the dissemination of fairly "user-friendly" simulation languages, a relatively high level of programming expertise is required to develop even a moderately complex computer simulation model. This requirement places the building of simulation models, if not their use, beyond the reach of researchers who lack the needed skills. While the policy planner or analyst does not necessarily have to be the member of the research team who commands the needed programming skills, the separation of technical skills from a theoretical and/or substantive

grasp of the subject matter increases the possibility of misunderstanding. One danger in such a situation is that purely technical considerations will take over in model building, leading to the development of "whiz-bang" models that fail to address the real underlying issues. A different problem is that even though theoretical or substantive considerations predominate, they may be inadequately represented in the model itself.

CLOSING THE GAP BETWEEN THEORISTS
AND PRACTITIONERS

Policy planners and analysts have frequently regarded social science theory as interesting but largely irrelevant to their own daily activities. Part of this perception stems from the abstract, nonspecific nature of social science theory, whereas the decisions planners and managers face are concrete and specific. Simulation can help close the gap between theorists and practitioners by juxtaposing the principles of social science theory with the specific organizational and environmental realities imposed by the real world. Computer simulation, then, allows the specific details that a practitioner must consider to be incorporated into an abstract model built on social science theory and principles. The power of the tool is that it not only can generate and expand theory, but can also apply theory to specific contexts and facilitate real-world decision making.

3

Designing a Computer Simulation: How to Build Your Own

Beginning a computer simulation may initially seem overwhelming. It is vital to recognize that building a model and running a simulation are as much art forms as they are explicitly stated, readily grasped sets of procedures. There are no hard and fast rules about how to formulate a problem, nor are there any ironclad formulas about the nature of the variables or parameters that will be included in the model. Modeling as an art form consists of an ability to analyze a problem, abstract its essential features, select and modify basic assumptions that characterize the system, enrich and elaborate the model until a useful approximation results, and then manipulate the model to obtain interesting, nonobvious results.

What constitutes a good computer simulation model? According to Little (1970), a good model is one that can be readily grasped by the user. Moreover, it is goal- or purpose-directed—not a mere toy. The results it produces possess face validity; while they may well be nonobvious, they are not absurd. The model is readily controllable and manipulable, and focuses attention on the key elements of the problem of interest. Finally, it is adaptable, in that it can be modified or updated, as well as evolutionary, in that from a simple early version it can be made more complex as the user's understanding of the problem becomes more sophisticated.

STEPS IN THE SIMULATION-BUILDING PROCESS

Morris (1967) offers several rules of thumb for initiating the model-building process. Among these guidelines are the suggestions that the modeler should begin with a clear statement about the objectives of the modeling exercise. This may seem too obvious even to mention, but it is remarkable how many models seem to be built purely for the sake of building a model, with little or no thought given to the uses of the model for addressing significant theoretical or policy issues.

After the objectives of the exercise have been clarified, a good second step is to factor the overall problem into more manageable components. Indeed, one of the strengths of modeling is that it literally forces the researcher to decompose the problem and to make explicit the connections among its various parts. Morris also recommends working through a concrete numerical example of the problem rather than restricting oneself wholly to the realm of the abstract.

Establishing and sticking with a consistent set of symbols is crucial. So is writing down the obvious, much of which will be explicitly incorporated into the model in the form of assumptions, parameters, and algorithms. Then, if a promising model begins to emerge, one should try to enrich it. A model that does not seem to be working out as intended, on the other hand, should usually be simplified rather than enriched, since it is rarely fruitful to embellish a model that is fundamentally flawed.

Simplification involves such steps as converting variables into constants, eliminating or combining variables, and possibly assuming linear rather than nonlinear relationships. Simplification also may involve building stronger assumptions and restrictions into the model, or limiting the boundaries of the problem. Enrichment, of course, involves just the opposite—turning constants into variables, including new variables, or disaggregating existing ones, jettisoning the often simplistic assumption of linearity, reducing the restrictiveness of assumptions, and expanding the scope of the problem.

More comprehensively, we can outline the stages through which a computer simulation passes by summarizing Shannon's (1975) description:

System definition. At this stage, the modeler determines the boundaries, restrictions, and variables that define the system.

Model formulation. The modeler then reduces or abstracts the real system to a contingency table or logical flow diagram.

Data preparation. The modeler then identifies the data requirements of the model (e.g., to provide initial values for key variables) and records these data.

Model translation. At this point the modeler "programs" the model (i.e., describes it in computer-readable code).

Validation. As was noted earlier, validation consists of comparing data about the real system and the system as simulated, permitting the modeler to determine how confidently inferences based on the simulation can be applied to the real system.

Strategic planning. Once satisfied that the model is valid, the modeler sets about designing an experiment for the model that will yield the desired information.

Tactical planning. Having determined the overall strategy, the modeler determines more specifically how the various test runs involved in the experimental design are to be executed.

Experimentation. The modeler then executes the simulation in order to generate the desired information by performing sensitivity analysis.

Interpretation. Of course, the outcomes of the simulation do not speak for themselves. Rather, they must be interpreted in terms of their bearing on the underlying issues that motivated the simulation exercise.

Implementation. Particularly in policy-oriented simulations, the interpreted results can be put to actual use.

Documentation. Finally, all salient aspects of the simulation model need to be recorded in order to facilitate replication and extension of the simulation exercise.

As is true of many procedures that are defined as a series of steps, the list of steps often makes the procedure seem more formidable—or even forbidding—than it really is. Many experienced simulators may not even realize that they routinely go through several of the steps in Shannon's description. As one grows more adept at simulation, some of these become second nature rather than conscious procedures. However, it certainly would be wise for the beginner explicitly to work through each step.

Philosopher of science Abraham Kaplan (1964) has decried what he calls the "law of the instrument": "Give a small boy a hammer and he will immediately find that everything he encounters needs pounding." This tendency is well known in social science, where researchers often seem to approach a problem not because it is theoretically important or socially significant, but rather because it seems a likely candidate for hammering. Computer simulation provides the analyst with an extremely adaptable set of tools, but in order to realize the potential of simulation for theory building and policy planning and analysis, one must have a secure grasp on the substance of the problem being studied. A highly sophisticated simulation based on a fundamental misunderstanding of the underlying issue is unlikely to advance, and may even retard, theoretical progress and policy development. Sometimes, however, the modeler can err in the opposite direction, by trying to simulate too much at once. Accordingly, it is preferable to design a model around the core questions to be answered, rather than trying to imitate the real system in full detail.

CHOOSING THE TYPE OF
COMPUTER SIMULATION TO USE

Much of the power of computer simulation stems from the flexibility of the technique. Yet this flexibility also can lead to confusion when one is first learning how to build models. Because so many different types of simulation are possible, the analyst faces many choices. This poses many opportunities, but these can be opportunities to go wrong unless the analyst understands the implications of the choices he or she must make. The following are among the most important of these choices.

Structural or Behavioral

The first choice is what to model. The researcher may probe either processes, or structures, or both. Generally, behavioral models focus on the actions of individuals, while structural models examine the impact of organizational or institutional configurations. This distinction is similar to that among various units of analysis in traditional social science research. In selecting a unit of analysis, the researcher decides at what level to collect empirical data. The dependent, independent, and control variables must be defined and measured at the level selected as the unit of analysis. Data not pitched at the appropriate level of analysis do not come directly into play. For example, a computer simulation of how a voter chooses between two candidates in a presidential election in the United States would clearly be behavioral, and the impact of structural factors such as the number and types of parties and the nature of the electoral laws would not come into play, since they would in effect be constant parameters. On the other hand, a simulation of the impact of at-large versus ward-based city council systems upon minority representation on city councils clearly is structural, and the attributes and attitudes of individual voters, which play a central role in the behavioral model of vote choice, would play no direct role in this structural model.

In computer simulation, the selection of a structural or behavioral model is based on the analyst's understanding of the primary research question. This means that before the simulation can proceed very far, one must devote a great deal of thought to stating the research question as precisely as one can. Of course, even after one has settled on a particular type of simulation—structural or behavioral—one can still incorporate other types of information, because assumptions and parameters can relate to structure, behavior, or both. For example, the primary research question, independent variables, and dependent variables might all be stated in terms of organizational structure. Assumptions about individual behavior, however, can be incorporated into a model of the organization.

Static or Dynamic

While computer simulation models can include an explicit time element, they do not necessarily do so. In particular, models that probe structure alone are more likely to be static, while behavioral models are more likely to be dynamic. The ability to monitor processes over time, which constitutes one of the strengths of computer simulation, is lost in static modeling, but many of the other advantages, such as the ability to incorporate great complexity, still hold.

Deterministic or Stochastic

Deterministic models include no random variance. Every specific set of input conditions produces one, and only one, unambiguous set of results. Given these conditions, the outcomes generated by the model *must* follow; if one ran the model a thousand times, one would produce the very same result a thousand times. Stochastic models, on the other hand, include algorithms with probabilistic calculations, and therefore deliver results that are probabilistic in nature. For example, in the behavioral model of vote choice mentioned above, one might assign a 60% probability of voting for Candidate A to a particular type of voter. This means that there is no guarantee that voters of this type will vote for Candidate A, only that in a specific instance each one of them should have a .6 chance of doing so. Sometimes people do the unexpected, like voting for Candidate B when their probability of doing so was only .4. This is because the behavior of voters who, after all, are humans, cannot be predicted with certainty. Accordingly, in one run-through of a stochastic model of voting we might find that a given voter of this type is predicted to vote for Candidate A, but that in the very next run-through of the model she is predicted to vote for Candidate B. Such variance is a direct consequence of the stochastic or random element in the model, which represents the nondeterministic nature of the process being simulated.

It follows that in stochastic models, a particular run-through for a given set of input conditions is only one member of a sample of runs for that set of input conditions; on the next run-through, the outcome could well turn out differently, given the presence of the random element. How large the sample must be is a function of the amount of variability built into the model, the researcher's tolerance for error in forecasting, and the confidence level desired.

It becomes vital to include stochastic variance when modeling a process that is known to be probabilistic, or when great uncertainty exists. One subset of stochastic models, those employing the "Monte Carlo" method, imitate random processes whose associated variables have unknown distributional properties. The inclusion of stochastic variation, however, makes it more difficult to draw unambiguous conclusions, so unless one has a specific reason to include a stochastic component, deterministic models are preferable.

When either a uniform or a normal distribution is used to simulate a stochastic phenomenon, then the average outcome for that phenomenon across multiple runs is the mean. A uniform distribution is one with an equal number of observations all across the range of values, while a normal distribution is the familiar symmetrical bell-shaped curve; in either case, the mean of the distribution adequately depicts the central tendency of the distribution. If the stochastic variable does not interact with or affect other variables in the model, nothing is gained from adding the stochastic variation and conducting multiple runs, because the overall result will be identical to holding the stochastic variable constant at its mean. In such cases, deviations from the expected value amount to sampling error (random error distributed about the mean) and hence are an undesirable nuisance.

If the stochastic variable does interact with other variables in the model, however, then there is reason to incorporate the stochastic disturbances, because holding the phenomenon constant as a parameter at its mean value would fail to capture these interactive effects. For example, one could assume (1) that the decision maker whose choice of candidates in a national election is the subject of a simulation is from either the United States or Germany, and (2) that the American voter responds electorally to the performance of the national economy in a manner consistent with the normal distribution while the German voter responds in a manner consistent with a bimodal distribution. The pairing of these two assumptions introduces an interaction between the nationality of the decision maker and the underlying repertoire from which the decision maker's response will be drawn. It would obviously be simpler to assume that Americans and Germans respond in the same way, but the modeler may not consider that assumption appropriate. In that case, the modeler will have to decide on a tradeoff between simplicity and reality. In general, the modeler must carefully consider whether the closer approximation to reality gained by adding stochastic variation compensates for the additional complexity and error such inclusion entails.

Interactive or Batch

In an interactive model, the model's performance periodically is adjusted to account for input supplied by the modeler while the model is running. That is, the model will stop in midstream and pose a question to the modeler. When it receives the modeler's answer, it will proceed accordingly. In non-interactive or batch models, all behavioral subroutines are spelled out beforehand, in the computer code. No human input is required, once the initial decisions about appropriate levels of independent variables for testing have been specified. A general idea of the difference between interactive and batch models can be conveyed by imagining a simulation of a chess match. In the interactive mode, a human player might be pitted against "the machine," and the player would be repeatedly asked to specify what move he or she wants to make. In the batch mode, the purpose might be to simulate a match between two great chess masters—say, Fischer and Karpov. The modeler would program, as fully and accurately as possible, a model of Fischer's strategies and tactics, and of Karpov's as well, and would then stand by and observe while the two simulated chess masters waged their competition.

Interactive models, sometimes called gaming models, have been gaining in popularity; indeed, the immensely popular video games that youngsters spend so many hours playing are, whether the players know it or not, interactive. That is, the player continuously or intermittently, depending on the nature of the game, supplies input that affects the subsequent course of the game. In interactive models, some behavioral subroutines are not specified in computer code. Rather, a participant or subject is queried by the program for input at appropriate places. Clearly, such models are stochastic, since the output derived from any single replication depends, in part, upon inputs supplied by the person responding. Since these inputs differ from one run to the next, the model's outputs vary as well. Accordingly, drawing trustworthy conclusions about the major research hypothesis on the interactive models requires a number of replications with different subjects.

Continuous or Discrete

Continuous variables can assume any value within a prespecified or an infinite range, while discrete variables can assume only a limited array of values representing different categories. The value of a continuous variable has inherent meaning, but the numerical value of a discrete variable may be nothing more than an indicator of a particular category; for example, in a racial classification a value of 1 may designate Asians, 2 blacks, and 3 whites, but these numeric values merely are place holders, with no mathematical meaning.

The nature of the simulation determines the type of variables used. Often the characteristics of variables are related to the degree of aggregation in the model. Continuous variables, such as gross national product per capita or violent crimes per 100,000 population, are commonly used in the analyses of social, political, and economic phenomena. For example, one might build a structural model of crime, in which the dependent variable is the rate of crimes against persons per 100,000 population. Behavioral models, however, often employ discrete variables, such as dichotomies representing whether something does or does not occur. For example, one might build a behavioral model of crime in which the dependent variable is whether a particular person, placed in a particular set of circumstances, does or does not commit a crime against another person.

Variables in computer simulation models can change in four ways: (1) in a continuous fashion at any point in time; (2) in a discrete fashion at any point in time; (3) in a continuous fashion, but only at certain points in time; or (4) in a discrete fashion, but only at certain points in time (Emshoff and Sisson, 1970; Pidd, 1984). As this formulation makes explicit, change in a particular phenomenon can be modeled as either discrete or continuous. Consider, for example, a subway system that contains trains that move from station to station picking up and depositing passengers at each stop. Many of the events in this system are discrete, such as when the train stops at a station, the doors open, passengers enter and exit, doors close, and so on. A discrete simulation of this process would focus on system change that transpires after a particular discrete event occurs, such as a stop at a given station or a temporary system shutdown. By contrast, in a continuous change model of the subway system, the values of variables would change continuously as the simulation progresses. Such variables might include the speed of the train as it moves from station to station, first accelerating and then decelerating. These variables would be represented by differential equations that, at least in theory, permit the modeler to calculate the train's speed at any particular point in time.

The primary social science users of continuous change models are economists modeling the behavior of economic systems via sets of differential equations, in much the same way as engineers model physical systems. With the exception of economists and some experimental psychologists modeling biological responses to various stimuli, most social scientists employ discrete change simulations.

Recursive or Quasi-Equilibrium

Dynamic models can follow one of two approaches. In the recursive approach, the state of the system at a given time is derived wholly within the model, from conditions at earlier times; the value of each variable in the system at any point in time is a function of previous values of variables within the system. For more complex situations, however, such as models of the whole economy, a quasi-equilibrium approach often is followed. This approach is better suited when interactions among variables are many and complex and when the time interval being simulated is long (such as a year). In such circumstances, it is unsafe to assume that no newly emergent forces are acting on the system; in other words, the implicit or explicit *ceteris paribus* (other things being equal) assumption is less likely to hold in more complex models with longer time frames. Various interactions, such as that between wages and prices in different submarkets or that between savings and investment rates in the macroeconomy, are represented by a set of simultaneous equations that must be solved for each time period. These solutions can be quite lengthy. Typically, the researcher examines the model results after each time period and decides whether to adjust key coefficients based on his or her judgment or on information not included in the model.

HANDLING TIME

Computer simulation allows time to be speeded up, so that weeks, months, and even years can be modeled with seconds, or at most, minutes of computer time, or to be slowed down, so that the passage of a mere nanosecond can be broken into virtually endless components. The flow of time can be handled in several ways (Pidd, 1984).

Time Slicing

This simple approach involves moving time forward in equal intervals. In time slicing, the model is regularly examined and updated. For a time slice of length s, the updating of the model occurs at time $(t + s)$ to represent changes occurring in the interval $[t$ to $(t + s)]$; this simply means, for example, that if $s = 5$ minutes and $t = 10$ minutes, the updating based on changes occurring between the 10th and 15th minute occurs at the end of the 15th minute.

Obviously, this approach requires that before executing the simulation, the modeler must specify an appropriate interval for time slicing. The length of the time slice will vary according to the process being simulated. Since supertankers move slowly, a reasonable interval for simulating the flow of traffic into and out of a supertanker terminal might be one hour, while an appropriate time slice for simulating air traffic at a busy airport might be half a minute or less. If the time interval is too long, the outcome observations will be too coarse and the desired degree of detail will be lost. If the time interval is too short, the model will be reexamined needlessly often and long-term processes may be obscured.

Next Event Technique

Many systems undergo slack periods of varying lengths during which no change occurs. Time in these systems may be modeled via a "next event" approach. With this approach, the time interval is permitted to vary, and the model is examined and updated only when a known system change is due. For example, this approach might be used to simulate activity in a manufacturing process in which tasks of varying and known length are performed in a fixed order. The model would be updated only when one task is completed and another is scheduled to start.

Unlike the time-slicing approach, the next event approach automatically adjusts system monitoring to periods of low and high activity, thereby avoiding wasteful rechecking when nothing of significance is occurring. It also records all significant events that occur within the system. Its primary potential disadvantages are that it requires more comprehensive information about the system and that the simulated time moves in fits and starts rather than flowing smoothly.

GENERATING RANDOM NUMBERS AND RANDOM VARIATES

Random variates are used in computer models in order to permit the modeler to make statements about the results of a nondeterministic model. Two steps are involved in incorporating stochastic disturbances into a simulation model (Mihram, 1972; Emshoff and Sisson, 1970). The first is the creation of random numbers that are totally independent of the simulation model. A procedure for generating random numbers must meet several criteria. A procedure that can produce numbers having any of k different values produces random numbers if each of these values has a probability of occurrence of $1/k$ (i.e., if each value is equally likely to occur). Each new value also must be completely independent of any previous values produced by the random number generator. More formally, the randomly generated numbers are uniformly distributed and independent.

In most computer simulations, programs based on recursive mathematical relationships are used to generate streams of random numbers. Random number generators based on mathematical relationships, however, are not truly random, since the sequence is entirely deterministic. From the viewpoint of the user and the output, the "pseudorandom" sequences so generated are indistinguishable from random sequences based on physical sources, such as a spinning roulette wheel, a tossed die, or a flipped coin, with one exception. The exception is that submitting the same inputs into the mathematically-based pseudorandom number generator will cause exactly the same output to emerge every time. Thus, if the pseudorandom series reaches a point where its input begins to be repeated, the sequence of "random" numbers being outputted will be the same as the sequence generated previously.

A number of pseudorandom number generators are available. Many introductory statistics texts include tables of random numbers, and if one simply needed to embed a short pseudorandom numerical sequence in a program, such a table would be an appropriate place to look. However, a much better way for the modeler to proceed in general is to generate pseudorandom numbers within the framework of the computer program. This is easy to do in most programming languages; for example, the most popular and one of the simplest programming languages, BASIC, provides a predefined function (referred to as RND) that generates numbers from a pseudorandom sequence.

The second step is the translation of the random numbers into random variates, a process in which the researcher uses a random number to create an observation from the distribution assumed to describe the probabilistic nature of the random variable being created. The random variates are defined in terms of probability statements formed by calculations using the cumulative distribution function—a nonnegative, monotonically nondecreasing function (i.e., one that never drops below the current level) bounded by zero and one. Various methods for converting a random number into a random variate with a specified distribution are employed, though here we simply note that such methods exist and leave their exposition to more advanced treatments cited in the bibliography of this book. Of course, the distributions themselves can vary widely. Most familiar is the normal or Gaussian distribution, which approximates a bell-shaped curve, the practical importance of which stems from the central limit theorem, which states that if a random variable arises as the sum of a large number of relatively insignificant contributions, then its probability density function will be Gaussian. But the normal distribution by no means exhausts the range of possibilities. Two other especially important distributions are the uniform and the binomial. A continuous random variable is uniform if, over a specified interval, it is equally likely to take on any value; therefore, in a uniform distribution, unlike a normal distribution, extremely high or low values are just as likely as middle values are. The binomial distribution, on the other hand, is the probability function of a series of independent "Bernoulli trials" having a particular number of successes. Bernoulli trials are repeated performances of a random experiment following the same basic pattern. A sequence of trials occurs so that (1) for each trial, there are only two possible outcomes ("success" and "failure"); (2) the probabilities of success and failure on each trial remain constant across trials; and (3) the trials are carried out independently, so that the outcome of any single trial does not affect the outcome of other trials. Beyond the normal, the uniform, and the binomial, many other types of distribution are available, including the geometric, negative binomial, multinomial, Poisson, gamma, lognormal, and beta. Again, we leave discussion of these and other distributions for more advanced texts, cautioning novices, in particular, to bear in mind that the distributional assumptions a modeler makes have a great bearing on the outputs from a simulation. For example, there is strong warrant to represent intelligence as being randomly distributed in a model of educational achievement of the general population. But if the same model assumed that income, too, is normally distributed, then the simulation results would almost certainly misstate the likely educational outcomes.

EXPERIMENTAL DESIGN
IN COMPUTER SIMULATION

Experimental design plays a central role in computer simulation. A computer simulation is, in essence, an abstract experiment, and the same principles that guide the development of laboratory-based experiments guide the development of computer simulations as well. The design of the computer-based experiment determines the success of the experiment in answering the primary questions of the research (Shannon, 1975).

Unlike real-world experiments, however, computer experiments are less concerned with constituting a sample or defining a particular set of data points, replicating experimental conditions, or controlling the variability of confounding factors. The modeler does not worry about forming an actual observational sample, since he or she is engaging in a "mind experiment." Moreover, as we have noted, while it is vital for the modeler to document the model well enough to facilitate replication and extension, constructing actual experimental conditions is not a consideration. The abstractness of computer models, and the fact that conditions are specified through computer code rather than being physically manipulated or held constant, allows these factors to be "controlled" purely by fiat.

Once the modeler has determined the dependent variable and has identified the factors that seem to affect it, each factor is built into the simulation model in one of three ways: (1) it can be held constant, becoming part of the boundary conditions through being a contro variable or parameter; (2) it can be allowed to vary without being controlled, becoming part of experimental "error" through being a random variate; or (3) it can be specified and systematically manipulated in the experiment, becoming an independent variable. The basic structure of the computer model then can be identified. The relevant design considerations include the following.

The Number of Factors to Be Varied

One must determine how many independent variables are to be included in the simulation. In the simplest type of design, the single-factor experiment, only one factor is varied. In progressively more complex designs, more and more factors are varied. Of course, the factors to be varied are determined by the modeler's substantive interests.

Well-designed factorial experiments are symmetric, in that each level of a given factor or independent variable is combined in turn with every level of the other factors in the experiment. Factorial designs are preferable to a "one factor at a time" approach for several interrelated reasons. They greatly facilitate interpretation of the independent and joint effects of the various factors. They permit the analyst to estimate the effect of a particular independent variable at several levels of other factors or independent variables, clarifying the extent to which conclusions hold over a wide range of conditions. More generally, they are easy to use and interpret.

The Number of Levels (Values)
to Be Used for Each Factor

Setting the number of values for each factor in the simulation involves the analyst in such issues as whether a variable is conceived as an interval or ratio scale (e.g., age in years) or as a nominal or ordinal scale (e.g., Protestant, Catholic, Jew; strongly disagree, disagree, agree, strongly agree); whether the levels of various factors are to be manipulated systematically or randomized; whether nonlinear effects are to be permitted; and whether all factors are to be set to an equal number of levels to achieve a balanced design.

With regard to level of measurement, nominal and ordinal variables can be assigned quantitative values (1, 2, 3, and so on) for the sake of convenience, but these numerical designations are essentially arbitrary. For ordinal variables, where ranking matters (e.g., first, second, third . . . , or excellent, good, fair . . .), the assigned integers within the simulation may correspond to the rank. However, the integers representing the ordinal variable in the simulation do not convey the same notions of distance that they would if the variable were conceived as being measured at the interval level.

The range of interest is of concern when dealing with continuous factors. If these variables are of interval level, then the numbers used to represent them in the simulation convey distance as well as rank. If these factors are assumed to be measured at the ratio level, their representation in the simulation conveys both distance and absolute magnitude. The design of the simulation is simplified by setting and testing continuous or quantitative variables at a few selected levels of interest throughout the range of possibilities, rather than setting and testing here at every possible point on the continuous scale. This way of treating continuous independent variables corresponds to the way they typically are handled in real-world experiments as well.

How many levels should the researcher select for continuous independent variables? Unlike nominal variables, where the number of levels or categories typically is obvious on the basis of theory or substantive concerns, the number of levels to be set for continuous variables is a matter for careful judgment. If the researcher is interested only in linear effects, then two levels of the continuous variables at the extremes of the range of interest might prove adequate as a means of conveying the overall impact of the factor. If the researcher is interested in nonlinear effects, then the number of levels selected should exceed the number of suspected dimensions of nonlinearity by at least one. For example, if quadratic effects, which require two dimensions, are suspected, then three levels of the independent variable must be selected. If cubic effects, which require three dimensions, are suspected, then four levels of the continuous independent variable must be selected. This correspondence of the number of dimensions in the suspected effect and the number of levels selected for a continuous quantitative variable results from the number of independent contrasts that can be made and the points necessary to define a function.

As in real-world experiments, analysis of output data is simplified greatly if the levels of a quantitative variable are set at equal intervals. In practice, two levels typically are set at the extreme points of range of interest, and intermediate points between the two extremes are set so that the intervals between them are equal.

Symmetrical experimental designs offer several analytical advantages over asymmetrical ones, especially if the number of levels of each variable is small—say two or three. A symmetrical design is achieved by using an equal number of levels for each independent variable.

The number of cells in a simulation model is calculated in the same fashion as the number of cells in other types of experimental designs. The total number of cells can be expressed as the product of the number of levels for every factor in the design. Thus, for example, in a design with four independent variables, each of which can assume three levels, the total number of cells, k, is:

$$k = 3 \times 3 \times 3 \times 3 = 81$$

If the design is asymmetric, with two of the independent variables assuming two levels while the other two assume three levels, then the total number of cells is:

$$k = 2 \times 2 \times 3 \times 3 = 36$$

Plainly, increasing the number of variables or the number of levels rapidly escalates the total number of cells in the design. In general, if $V_1, V_2, V_3 \ldots V_n$ are the number of values that independent variables 1 through n assume, then the total number of cells in the design is:

$$k = V_1 \times V_2 \times V_3 \times \ldots V_n$$

In a deterministic model, the number of cells determines the total number of data points or observations. In the first example above, the simulation would contain a total of 81 "cases" (that is, 81 different combinations of values of the independent variables), while in the second example, the total number of cases would be 36. In a model with stochastic variance, the number of cells determines the number of samples that must be generated, because a sample consisting of several observations must be drawn for each cell. If it were decided to draw a sample of 10 observations per cell, then in the first example the total number of cases would be 810 (81 cells with 10 observations per cell), while in the second example there would be 360 (36 cells multiplied by 10 observations per cell).

The Completeness of the Factorial Design

In complex factorial designs, where there are many independent variables, each of which can assume many levels, the number of cells in the design can be quite large. In stochastic models in particular, where a sample must be drawn from each cell, the total number of computer runs that must be undertaken for complete execution of the entire factorial design can be enormous.

In such situations, it may be desirable to simplify matters by cutting back on the full factorial design and instead identifying and modeling only the most important subset of independent variable values influencing the dependent variable. If the researcher is not interested in some particular combinations of independent variables, then considerable information can be obtained from a fractional replication, or a fractional factorial design. This is a reduced experimental design from the full factorial design. Only a fraction (such as $1/2$, $1/4$, or $1/8$) of the total number of combinations is explored. The researcher designs a series of short experiments that use a few runs to rapidly screen a larger number of independent variables for their effect upon the dependent variable. On the basis of these preliminary results, the researcher selects and concentrates on the more significant independent variables in subsequent computer runs.

Determining Sample Size

In stochastic models, the number of observations is determined in part by the size of the sample to be drawn from each cell in the design. Several considerations are important in determining sample size (see Lipsey, 1990). Among these are how large a shift in the dependent variable the researcher wants to be able to detect, how much variability is built into the model, how much risk of reaching an incorrect conclusion (falsely accepting or rejecting the null hypothesis) the researcher is willing to assume, and how the dependent variables are distributed. Sample size can be practiced either prior to actually running the model or while the model is in operation, using results generated by the model.

Using the central limit theorem. If the responses of the model are assumed to be independent and normally distributed, then sample size can be determined prior to running the model, with the aid of the central limit theorem. If the researcher wants to estimate the true population mean within a specified confidence interval and knows the population variance of the dependent variable, then the central limit theorem will yield the desired sample size. When the population variance is unknown, as is typically the case, then an estimate of it can be obtained from prior studies, a pilot study or runs, or a preliminary sample.

Using Tchebycheff's Theorem. If the distribution in the underlying population cannot safely be assumed to be normal, then Tchebycheff's Theorem of Inequality, which makes no assumptions about normality, can be used instead of the central limit theorem. One pays a price for relinquishing the assumption of normality, however, because the required sample size generated by Tchebycheff's Theorem is invariably considerably larger than that generated by the central limit theorem.

Sample size with Bernoulli variables. Simulations often are designed with a proportion, fraction, or percentage as the primary dependent variable. In an industrial setting, for example, interest may center on the percentage of products that are defective, while in a national policy setting the issue may be the proportion of weapons that would be destroyed under a certain type of enemy attack. Such proportions, fractions, and percentages are aggregated forms of Bernoulli trials, in that the events on which they are based fall into one of two categories (e.g., success or failure; destroyed or not destroyed; present or absent). According to the Bernoulli Theorem, the difference between the proportion of successes in a certain number of trials and the true probability of a success in a single trial approaches zero as the number of trials approaches infinity. In a manner directly parallel to the central limit theorem, the Bernoulli Theorem can be used to estimate sample size.

Sample size with autocorrelated variables. To this point, the discussion of sample sizes has assumed that observations on the dependent variable are independent and uncorrelated. Yet often, in simulation, this is not the case: the current value of a dependent variable depends upon the past value of the same variable. For example, if one were simulating the trend over time in the size of the federal budget, one would surely want to recognize that the size of the federal budget does not fluctuate randomly from year to year; rather, this year's budget is based on last year's budget, so that over time the size of the budget at time t is likely to be a good predictor of the size of the budget at time $t + 1$.

The required sample size is quite sensitive to such autocorrelation. Two different approaches for dealing with autocorrelation are to divide the simulation run into two equal subgroups and treat each subgroup as a single independent observation, or to estimate an autocorrelation function and include its effects in the estimation of population parameters; the latter approach, after some fairly complex calculations, yields a minimum sample size.

Sample size determination within the model. As an alternative to predetermining sample size, one can determine confidence intervals for output values as they are generated in a simulation run, terminating the run when a predetermined confidence interval has been attained. There are various ways to include such an automatic stop procedure in a simulation model. Perhaps the least complicated of these is to run the simulation in two stages. In the first stage, one simply uses one's best guess of what the sample size should be. The results from the first stage (the mean of the dependent variable, the variance, and so on) are then used to calculate the sample size necessary to achieve the desired degree of precision. If the desired sample size is smaller than the size used in the first stage, nothing else need be done, since the sample is already larger than it needs to be. If the sample size needs to be larger than it was in the first stage, then the run is continued until the actual sample size reaches the desired level.

ADDRESSING CAUSAL QUESTIONS THROUGH COMPUTER SIMULATION

Just as the design of an experiment is crucial to the utility of an empirical study, the design of a computer simulation model determines its usefulness in answering major research questions. In empirical studies, research designs that fall short of an experimental design can only address correlational hypotheses bearing on the extent to which certain variables covary. Stronger hypotheses dealing with causation can be addressed in nonexperimental empirical designs only within the framework of assumptions that may or may not be appropriate to the problem at hand.

In computer simulation, by contrast, all three conditions for testing causal hypotheses can be built into the design. First, covariation between the independent and dependent variables can be analyzed and demonstrated. Second, changes in the independent variables can be manipulated so that they temporally precede changes in the dependent variables. Third, the possibility of spurious relationships between the independent and dependent variables can be eliminated by controlling for other factors affecting the dependent variables. Such control can be achieved by fixing such factors as parameters and holding their impact constant. This capability of a well-constructed computer simulation model to explore causal relationships heightens its power and flexibility as a research tool.

CONCLUSION

In this chapter we have described a number of different methods and techniques for conducting computer simulations. In concluding this chapter it is important to emphasize that computer simulation encompasses a broad array of strategies and tactics. There is no one best way to do computer simulation. There may well be a most appropriate approach to a particular substantive problem, but that is exactly our point: how one resolves the various methodological and technical choices one faces in computer simulation is a matter that cannot be decided in the abstract, apart from the substance of the problem in which one is interested. It is in the interplay between methodological and technical considerations, on the one hand, and substantive considerations, on the other, that the modeler faces his or her greatest challenge.

4

Technical Aspects of Simulation: Programming, Validating, and Analyzing a Computer Simulation Model

In this chapter, we consider a set of related operational issues concerning computer simulation modeling—issues concerning the actual construction of the simulation model and the validation and analysis of the simulation output. We begin with a consideration of programming languages, which modelers use to convey to the computer their instructions for how to carry out a simulation. Simulation (indeed, all tasks involving a computer) would be simpler if one could simply speak to the computer in one's natural language, instructing it, for example, "Create a random variable called X with 100 observations ranging from 0 to 1 drawn from a normal distribution." But at this point in the evolution of computer science, computers are still not adept at understanding natural human languages. Thus, in order to converse with a computer, modelers have to learn to use a language the computer is capable of understanding.

After surveying computer languages available for simulation, we turn to the issue of establishing the validity of a model—an issue that, as we shall see, has many subdimensions, some broad and abstract, some narrow and technical. Many validity-related issues ultimately can be decided through careful analysis of simulation results, and so next we consider systematic means of analyzing simulation results. Since simulations typically produce numerical output, often in copious quantity, this step is likely to involve statistical analysis. There is nothing peculiar about the quantitative output generated by simulations; numbers are simply numbers. But certain statistical techniques do tend to lend themselves especially well to simulation-based analyses, and we shall briefly review these.

Finally, we present an overview of the major types of errors that can crop up in computer simulation modeling, with an eye toward providing inexperienced modelers with some analytical tools that will help them avoid such errors when they begin to construct their own models.

56

PROGRAMMING LANGUAGES

Most of us, in everyday life, perform mathematical calculations in base 10 form. Digital computer software, however, represent information in binary (base 2) form or in some multiple of binary, such as octal (base 8) or hexadecimal (base 16). None of these representations is suitable for user simulations, unless the modeler is prepared to deliver complicated sets of instructions to the computer in an extremely lengthy series of zeroes and ones (in the binary case) or other digits. This approach is simply too far removed from the modeler's natural language for it to be of any use. Nor are assembler languages any more useful, for they are machine-oriented and usually are designed for a specific type of computer. By contrast, compiler languages are procedure- and problem-oriented, are not tied to a particular type of machine, and are "friendlier" to the user. Compiler languages are suitable for simulation, since they significantly decrease the amount of time needed to program a complex problem and lessen the probability of error in programming by reducing the number of statements needed to execute any particular operation.

For our purposes, compiler languages can be separated into two classes—general-purpose languages, such as ALGOL, BASIC, C, COBOL, FORTRAN, PASCAL, and PL/I, and special-purpose languages, including some specifically designed for simulation, such as DYNAMO, GASP, GPSS, SIMSCRIPT, and SIMULA. Simulations can be written in both general-purpose and special-purpose simulation languages (Shannon, 1975). Many microcomputer users have at least a rudimentary command of one general-purpose language, BASIC, which is supplied with many microcomputers. Many experienced programmers castigate BASIC for what they see as its inelegance and its encouragement of poor programming habits. In our own experience with computer simulation, however, BASIC has proven quite serviceable, and we believe that its easy accessibility makes it a reasonable starting place for newcomers to computer simulation.

Special-Purpose Languages

Special-purpose simulation languages often require less programming time than general-purpose languages. These languages typically provide error-checking techniques superior to those provided in general-purpose languages, as well as convenient procedures for expressing intermediate variables generated during a simulation execution and simulation output. Simulation languages may include easy procedures for establishing needed subroutines, and may automatically generate various types of requested statistical distributions. They also facilitate the collection and display of data produced during the run, and the control and allocation of memory during execution.

One disadvantage of simulation languages is that often they do not provide the modeler with a great deal of flexibility. They are designed to do one thing well, and so they tend to do other things poorly or not at all. There also are considerable start-up costs to learning and becoming adept in special-purpose languages, especially since many programmers and analysts are already familiar with and fairly skilled at general purpose languages, especially BASIC.

Several issues must be considered when selecting a programming language. Among these are whether or not intelligibly written users' manuals are available, and whether a compiler for the language is available for the computer being used for the simulation. If one intends to run the simulation on machines other than one's own, will the language run on them? The analyst also needs to consider the documentation available for the language, and whether it includes extensive error diagnostics. Also, is the language reasonably efficient in terms of organizing, programming, and debugging time as well as compiling and execution time? What are the financial costs associated with the language? Some languages are proprietary, so using them requires payment for installation, maintenance, and updating. Ease of learning the new language is an additional consideration. If the purchase of a special simulation language is being contemplated, are enough simulation studies planned to make the purchase worthwhile?

Beginners would be well advised not to commit themselves to a special simulation language until it becomes apparent that their interest in modeling will be long-lasting and that a particular language is best suited to their interest.

General-Purpose Programming Languages

General-purpose languages usually provide great flexibility, but by definition they are not specifically designed to perform a particular task. The trade-offs involved in use of special or general purpose programming languages are exactly the same as the trade-off between any multipurpose tool, like a Swiss Army knife, and another tool designed to perform a single function. One can perform simulations with a general-purpose language, but sometimes it may be more awkward to do so than it would be if one were using a special simulation language. Programmers and analysts may already be adept with a general-purpose language and familiar with its strengths, weaknesses, special facilities, and debugging approaches. However, since general-purpose languages are not specifically designed for simulation, they lack some of the built-in special features simulation languages often offer. Hence, programming a model with a general-purpose language rather than a simulation language may lengthen the programming time and amount of code needed.

It is not our purpose to teach readers how to write programs. Those who have no programming expertise will have to overcome this hurdle before they themselves can construct computer simulations and, for that matter, before they can participate in an informed manner in a simulation exercise for which someone else does the actual programming. Although programming initially may seem an overwhelming task, most general-purpose programming languages are actually fairly easy for most people to learn and use. Over time, the number of general-purpose compiler languages available for programming simulation models has greatly expanded. Several criteria can be used to evaluate these general-purpose languages (Tucker, 1986).

Expressivity. Expressivity refers to the ability of the language to convey the substantive meaning the programmer intends. Expressive languages allow algorithms to be expressed compactly, and facilitate structured programming through the use of such expressions as "while" loops and "if-then-else" statements.

Comprehensive definition. If a language is well defined, its syntax and semantics are free of ambiguity, internally consistent, and complete. Natural languages often are extremely ill-defined, so that a single utterance can take on entirely different meanings for different listeners. Moreover, it is difficult to convey certain ideas in some natural languages; for example, the German notion of *Gemütlichkeit* is essentially untranslatable into English. The same holds for programming languages. Certain procedures are difficult to perform in some languages, and others cannot be performed at all. Or the modeler may be taken by surprise by the results a given piece of computer code produces, because the rules of the language led the modeler to anticipate something quite different. Problems of inadequate definition are especially likely to occur early in the development of language, but it is also true that languages vary considerably in terms of how well defined they are for various purposes.

Data types and structures. The greater the variety of data values (integers, real numbers, strings, pointers, and so forth) and "non-elementary" collections of data values a general-purpose language supports, the better, as such variety enhances the flexibility of the language from the modeler's standpoint.

Modularity. The two aspects of modularity used in evaluating a general-purpose compiler language are its support for subprogramming and its capability for allowing programmer-defined operators and data types. Subprogramming refers to the ability to define independent procedures and functions (subprograms) and to communicate with the main program. For example, the modeler may plan to use the same set of commands at various points in a model, as would be the case if one wanted to draw values from a normal distribution several times in a given simulation. In such a case, it would be good programming practice to design a single module that draws values from a normal distribution, and to call up that module from various points in the program, rather than including the same set of commands in the model over and over again. Modular programming is extremely efficient. Moreover, just as the ability to isolate and swap modular components in a television set can help one diagnose why the set is not functioning properly, modular programming can be quite useful when one is trying to trace a programming error.

Portability. A portable language can be implemented on a variety of computers and is largely "machine-independent."

Efficiency. Efficient languages permit fast compilation and execution of programs.

Pedagogy. Other factors being equal, a language should be easy to teach and learn.

Generality. Even if it is used primarily for simulations, a general-purpose language obviously should be useful across a wide range of programming applications. BASIC programs, for example, are available for almost every application imaginable.

Some Prominent General-Purpose Languages

FORTRAN. Originated in 1954, FORTRAN (FORmula TRANslating System) is among the oldest and most durable of programming languages. It was developed for scientific and engineering applications, and is readily adaptable to simulation modeling. FORTRAN is highly efficient, with good modularity, portability, good definition, and pedagogy. FORTRAN's strength in scientific applications makes it a good general-purpose language for simulation modeling.

BASIC. BASIC has been, and remains, the primary programming language for users of microcomputers. It is easy to teach and learn. Its biggest drawback, until recently, has been low portability, because different brands of computers implemented slightly different dialects of BASIC. Increasingly, with the market dominance of IBM PCs and IBM clones, Microsoft BASIC has become a de facto standard. BASIC ranks lower in terms of definition than some other general-purpose languages.

PASCAL. PASCAL was developed in the early 1970s primarily for use in university computer science curricula. Because it was designed to instruct students in algorithm design and program construction, it ranks reasonably high in pedagogy. It also has achieved moderate use in mathematical, data processing, and artificial intelligence applications. It is well defined.

LISP. LISP (LISt Processor) was designed mainly for symbolic formula manipulation and has been widely used in artificial intelligence applications. It is unparalleled in its ability to express recursive algorithms that manipulate dynamic data structures. It also is well defined, with a high degree of modularity and expressivity, but it is harder to teach and learn than other languages.

For their efficiency, flexibility, pedagogy, and wide availability, BASIC and FORTRAN remain among the strongest general-purpose language candidates for social science simulation applications. As noted above, a number of special simulation languages also are available, but we would strongly advise novices to begin working with one of the general-purpose languages, especially if they have any experience with it or anticipate other, nonsimulation uses for it.

CONCEPTS OF MODEL VALIDATION

Once a computer simulation model has been constructed in whatever language the modeler finds most appropriate, model validation and verification remain as tasks.

The Issue of External Validity

External validity refers to the degree of homomorphism between one system and a second system it represents (Stanislaw, 1986). Homomorphism is similar, but not identical, to the criterion of isomorphism. The goal of abstraction is to map a complex, real-world n-dimensional system onto a less complex, abstract m-dimensional system, where $n > m$. Isomorphism, which would require that $m = n$, is an inappropriate criterion for the external validity of a simulation; requiring isomorphism would defeat the ability of the simulation to simplify reality through abstraction. Homomorphism, on the other hand, is a less stringent criterion. It involves correspondence in form or appearance without requiring perfect correspondence in structure.

The external validity of a computer simulation model is a function of how well the theory underlying the model represents the underlying phenomena, and how well the computer program represents the model.

Theory Validity

Because theories are necessarily abstract, they provide a selective reality rather than a comprehensive account of the truth. For any given set of conditions, a theory must predict a set of outcomes that is smaller than the total possible range of outcomes. Errors may arise from incomplete or inaccurate knowledge of the system about which the theory is being developed. If the universe is probabilistic rather than deterministic, theoretical predictive accuracy can never exceed some upper bound, since probability necessarily encompasses some prediction error (Petrinovich, 1979). Because theories are reductions from reality and the goal of theory building is to "lose" specific information for the sake of gaining general knowledge, the "trick" is to abstract without a significant reduction in explanatory power. All abstraction involves some loss of explanatory power; but how much loss is tolerable varies with the needs of the researcher.

Model Validity

A model is a theory whose component parts are represented by symbols that can be manipulated according to well-defined rules, typically those of mathematics or formal logic. The formalization and establishment of parameters for simulation models also may involve constraints upon validity. Some of these constraints result from limits of the formal rules in which the model is set; Euclidean geometry, for example, imposes different constraints from non-Euclidean geometry. Further, the constraints imposed by the formal mathematical or logical rules may not always be obvious or intuitive. Models also require more specific statements than do theories, and specificity may be a source of error. For example, a theory might posit that X is a function of Y, whereas a model might specify that X varies in inverse proportion to Y. The former statement, which subsumes the latter, may be correct, but the latter may not be. Achieving greater specificity then is not only a necessity for turning a theory into a model; it is also a source of "leakage" or misapplication from the theory. The famed Oracle of Delphi was never wrong for the simple reason that he never said anything specific enough to be pinned down. By the same token, one's chances of being correct are much greater when one says "It's going to be a nice day" than when one says "It's going to be 75 degrees and clear today." Theories often contain statements on the order of the former, but models must contain statements on the order of the latter.

Face Validity

A model that has high face validity is one that seems reasonable on its face to model users and others who are knowledgeable about the real system being simulated (Banks and Carson, 1984). Face validity is enhanced if the potential users of a model are involved in its conceptualization and construction. If the model is to be employed only by the researcher in order to address a specific set of research questions, then periodic feedback from others knowledgeable about the real system can be substituted for more widespread involvement in the construction of the model. Such feedback often proves invaluable in identifying deficiencies in the model.

Program Validity

Programming a model may engender an additional loss of validity. Since digital computers use discrete data to approximate continuous events, such as time, some error may result. Rounding errors may accumulate across iterations, and diminish validity. Other programming conventions may provide further constraints on validity. The impact of these errors in the "details" of programming cannot be overlooked, especially if it is important to generate a fairly precise set of output values. But the greater programming threat to validity lies in the difficulty of translating complex models into precise computer code. The opportunities for error abound—especially, as we have already noted, when the person writing the code is a technician who is not well versed in the substance of the model, or is a theorist who is not very sophisticated in the intricacies of programming. Even under the best of circumstances, though, programming a complex model is a challenging task that requires extreme care and continuous monitoring, for even a tiny and seemingly inconsequential error can alter fundamentally the output a program produces.

Validation of Model Assumptions

Structural assumptions are concerned with how the system operates. These assumptions usually simplify and abstract reality. In a model of queuing behavior in a bank, for example, structural assumptions might include whether customers form a single line or as many lines as there are cashiers; whether customers are served on a strict "first come, first served" basis or are permitted to change lines; and whether the number of cashiers is fixed or variable. *Data assumptions* are concerned with the nature and rate of flow of input, as well as the parameters of the model. In the bank queuing model, data assumptions would include interarrival times of customers during peak hours, interarrival times during slack hours, service times for commercial accounts, and service times for personal accounts.

If a random sample is used to develop input data, several steps are involved in analyzing the sample results, including identifying the appropriate probability distribution in the sample data and estimating the parameters of the hypothesized distribution to be used in the simulation model. A third step is the validation of the assumed statistical model by a goodness-of-fit test, such as chi-square test.

Validation of Input-Output Transformations

In order to be useful, a model should reflect a system's structure well enough to offer good predictions not just for one set of input data, but for a range of input data sets. Yet systems vary as to how much information exists to test the validity of input-output transformations. Typically, valid and reliable data for ranges of input values and corresponding output values are not available from the real-world system, restricting the researcher's ability to establish this type of validity; indeed, the unavailability of such data may be the very reason why the researcher has chosen to run a simulation in the first place rather than conducting a more standard empirical data analysis.

TESTS FOR MODEL VALIDATION

Since any type of invalidity poses a fundamental threat to computer simulation models, various means of testing for the presence of validity threats have been devised. Some of these testing methods are described below.

Face Validity

Under this "test," the researcher basically tries to be alert to major departures from expectations or to unusual program output. As long as the results are pretty much as expected, they are considered valid on their face, but when they fly in the face of the logic underlying the theory or when they contradict results reported elsewhere, their validity is considered suspect.

Some critics consider the criterion of face validity meaningless (Meir, Newell, and Pazer, 1969; Emshoff and Sisson, 1970). Critics argue that it is circular, contending that if the output from the process being simulated were known before the fact, there would be no need for a simulation in the first place. That is, if we are already convinced that we know what the answer is, it is pointless to look for evidence, since we will simply reject any counterevidence. On the other hand, face validity certainly can help establish program validity, and can be of immense aid in debugging. Even though complex models with interactive components can produce counterintuitive results, simple models or simple components of complex models should produce straightforward results. Thus a high degree of face validity is necessary but not sufficient to establish program validity.

If time and resources are available and if the values of model parameters and the specification of model structure cannot be based directly upon empirical data, then a panel of experts can be assembled to enhance and/or assess face validity. One procedure for eliciting expert opinion is the Delphi method (see Moore, 1987). In this iterative process, each participant's views are elicited, with no face-to-face interaction among participants. All information is channeled through a group coordinator, who informs the participants of the range of group opinion during the previous round of expert input and asks the participants to reconsider the inputs they provided during the preceding round.

The participants then offer new estimates. After a few iterations of this procedure, the range of opinion typically narrows and a consensus builds. Of course, the experts can be wrong, but procedures like the Delphi method can at least isolate points of consensus and dissension and can thereby help the modeler begin the modeling exercise with an informed set of estimates.

Face validity also can be gauged through sensitivity analysis, to determine whether the model behaves in the anticipated fashion when certain input values are altered. To use sensitivity analysis to examine face validity, the researcher must have some *a priori* notion of at least the direction, and preferably the magnitude as well, of change in output values when certain input values rise or fall. For example, even casual observation of people standing in line reveals that the amount of time spent waiting and the length of the line both increase as a function of the number of customers demanding service during a particular time period. Accordingly, the validity of a queuing model that failed to preserve this positive relationship between waiting time and line length, on the one hand, and number of customers demanding service, on the other, would be highly suspect.

If it is not possible to establish face validity by performing sensitivity tests with all the input variables in the model, one should attempt to do so with the most important variables in the model. This presumes, of course, that one has some prior notion of which are the most important variables in the model. If this is not the case, then there is reason to wonder whether one understands the phenomenon being modeled well enough to conduct the simulation.

Historical or Event Validity

Testing for event validity consists of inputting real-world independent variable conditions into the simulation model and seeing whether the model responds in the same way as the real-world system. Stanislaw (1986) suggests that event validity be employed during model or program development to determine appropriate parameter values and functional relationships. The model cannot be validated, however, with the same data that were used to build it. Separate, independent samples of data must be obtained. Split-sample, cross-validation techniques would require the program to be developed on a randomly selected portion of the available data, and verified on the remaining observations. Or a model developed on the basis of previously existing data can be verified on the basis of new data; for example, one might develop a simulation of the national economy with the aid of data from 1946 through 1985, and then use data from the 1986-1990 period to verify the model.

The Turing Test

In the Turing test of validity, trained judges are presented with output from the simulation model and with output from the real-world system and are asked to distinguish between the two. If they cannot do so at a level better than random chance, the model is declared valid.

This test has been criticized as the output from the simulation must frequently be edited or modified before being presented to judges, a process that introduces biases (Tuggle and Barron, 1980) and weakens its utility as a test of validity (Abelson, 1981; Revlin, 1981). Stanislaw (1986), however, sees the Turing test as measuring event validity, with human judges taking the place of statistical comparators.

The diversity and indeterminacy of each of these approaches to validity assessment suggest that there is no simple or conclusive way of demonstrating the validity of a computer simulation. Naturally, showing that a simulation can pass a number of different validity tests, any one of which is incomplete in itself, is a more impressive demonstration of validity than is showing that a simulation can pass a single test (Gerritsma and Smal, 1987). It is unfortunate but true that in many simulation studies no attempt is made to undertake even a single external validity test, let alone a battery of tests. Rather, most published research focuses on issues of internal validity and/or pedagogical value (Norris and Snyder, 1982). Greater attention to the issue of external validity is clearly warranted, for without external validity computer simulations are elegant but ultimately empty exercises.

Reasonableness Tests

There is no single or simple test to validate computer simulation models. Rather, various tests and procedures exist that collectively enhance one's confidence in a model as it is being constructed. Validation is an ongoing activity, occurring throughout the entire phase of model building and refinement.

Experts disagree over what is needed to demonstrate that a model is valid. Bulgren (1982) argues that before engaging in detailed statistical analyses of simulation output, a researcher must show that model results are "reasonable." That is, results must not violate common sense in terms of continuity, consistency, and degeneracy.

Continuity Tests

If continuity is present, small changes in the input values will cause observable change in the output values, and large changes in the input values will cause more observable change in the output values. Hence the output values are continuously responsive to input changes. If continuity is not present, changes in input values may leave the output values unchanged. Note that changes in input values should not always affect output values. There may, for example, be floors or ceilings for particular output variables. In a model intended to predict how fast one can run a mile, it would be reasonable to predict that the more one trains, the faster one will become; but it would be reasonable to predict that after a certain point has been reached, one would never go any faster. Thus the point is not to show that continuity necessarily exists in the relationship between input and output variables, but rather that the continuity relationship is reasonable.

Consistency Tests

Consistency is demonstrated by showing that similar cases (i.e., similar combinations of input values) produce similar results (i.e., similar output values). Demonstrating consistency also can involve showing that directional changes in input values are followed by changes in output values in the anticipated direction.

Degeneracy Tests

Models also can be tested for reasonableness in "degenerate" situations. This involves eliminating the effect of a component of the model (a parameter or an independent variable) and then checking to see whether the simulation performs as if the removed component has, indeed, been eliminated. Models that do not eliminate the effects of a removed feature do not accurately represent degenerative situations.

STATISTICAL TESTS FOR ANALYZING SIMULATION RESULTS

It is not our purpose to present a primer of statistical analysis. For one thing, many introductory treatments of statistical methods have been written expressly for social scientists and are readily available

For another, while statistical analysis of simulation data frequently is useful, it is not always necessary. One can imagine, for example, a simulation designed to produce a single number, but it is doubtful that one would wish to conduct a statistical analysis of a single number. For example, one might wish to predict how the nine members of the United States Supreme Court would vote on a test of the constitutionality of the War Powers Act. In a simulation-based analysis, a researcher could use assumptions about the preferences and motivations of each Justice to predict the vote breakdown—5-4, 6-3, or whatever. Since that prediction is the entire point of the exercise, there is no reason to conduct any statistical analysis. Even if the researcher went on to rerun the simulation model on the new assumption that, say, a particular member of the Supreme Court were replaced by a new member with different preferences and motivations, again the model would simply produce a single vote breakdown.

It is only when the matters are more complex that statistical analysis comes into play. Such complex circumstances include the following:

- *When the researcher is probing the effects of a large number of values of each input variable.* For example, one might build a model of the impacts of age (expressed in years) and level of education (also expressed in years) on adults' participation in community organizations. In such a model, one could have 70 or more different ages and 15 or more different levels of education— too many to be handled without some statistical treatment.
- *When the model contains a large number of input variables.* For example, one might build a comprehensive model of career choices that takes into account a welter of family background factors, life experiences, personal traits and preferences, and broader social circumstances—too many to keep track of without some statistical treatment.
- *When attention centers on the interactive effects of various combinations of input variables.* If one's model contains only two input variables and each variable is assumed to contribute in an additive fashion to some output variable, then one has a fairly simple task in terms of analysis and interpretation. If, however, one assumes that the two input variables interact in some fairly complex manner, then the scope of the analysis and interpretation quickly expands to a point that some statistical treatment becomes necessary. Assume, for example, that a model of the salary impacts of race and gender assumed (1) that blacks would be at a disadvantage

compared to whites, and (2) that women would be at a disadvantage compared to men, but (3) that black women would be at an advantage compared to all other groups. Clearly, the task of analyzing this interactive model is more complex than that of analyzing a simpler, additive model. As more variables with more complex interactions are brought into the model, the task becomes far more complex, and the possibility of proceeding solely via informal comparison falls by the wayside; formal statistical analysis becomes the only real possibility.

- *When many different output variables are being considered.* A two-factor model of career choice would be easy to handle in a non-statistical fashion. The results of a two-factor model of career choice, regional choice, residential choice, spousal choice, and friendship choice would be more difficult to present and compare without some statistical treatment.

- *When the issue is whether a given change in an output variable is too large to be attributed to chance fluctuations.* For example, a stochastic model of vote choice may generate the prediction that the likelihood of a certain type of voter selecting a certain type of candidate is .48, while the likelihood of a somewhat different type of voter selecting such a candidate is .54. What should one make of this difference? A first step in answering this question might be to determine whether such a difference is statistically significant (i.e., whether the hypothesis that it reflects chance fluctuations can confidently be rejected). That, of course, is a question that demands an appropriate statistical treatment.

- *When the researcher needs a probability estimate to be associated with the outcome generated by the simulation model.* One may wish to simulate not just the most likely outcome in a given set of circumstances, but also the probability of that outcome. It is one thing to predict that, for example, a nuclear war is unlikely to occur in a given set of conditions; however, whether the predicted likelihood is .000000049 or .49 is something else again. To the extent that one wishes to associate such probability estimates with the model's outcomes, one will be led toward a statistical treatment of the data.

So under a variety of circumstances, the researcher will need to employ some statistical techniques to analyze and present the results of the computer simulation modeling exercise. These techniques can range from the simplest—say, the calculation of a mean or the calculation of a percentage—to the most complex—say, the testing of a large-scale multivariate model. The analysis can be undertaken for purely *descriptive* purposes, or, if generalization to some broader population is intended (as often is the case in stochastic modeling), it can have a *probabilistic* or *inferential* thrust. In any event, *there is nothing peculiar about the statistical techniques that are used to analyze simulation data.* As noted earlier, the researcher needs a good all-around grasp of statistical techniques in order to (1) select the technique that is most appropriate, given the particular data configuration posed by the simulation output; and (2) ensure that once the appropriate technique has been chosen, it will be competently employed.

Within certain social science disciplines and subdisciplines, certain statistical techniques have gained favored status. The standard econometric tool, for example, is the multiple regression model along with its countless variations, while psychologists tend to favor analysis of variance- and covariance-related techniques. These choices make a great deal of sense in light of the types of problems that researchers in a given discipline typically consider. Psychologists, for example, tend to run experiments in which the treatment factors constitute nominal-level variables while the outcomes of the experiment are measured on interval scales. For this data configuration, the analysis of variance model is highly appropriate. Economists, on the other hand, tend to examine over-time relationships in variables like the demand for some good and the price of the good, both measured on interval scales. For this data configuration, time-series regression models are highly appropriate.

The difficulty, to return to a point made briefly earlier, is that social scientists too often conceptualize a problem to fit the statistical model with which they are most familiar rather than finding the statistical model that is best suited to the problem as they conceptualize it—another instance of Kaplan's (1964) "law of the instrument." One implication is virtually inescapable: Because the researcher needs to be in command of *appropriate* statistical technology and since computer simulation modeling closely parallels *experimental design,* the researcher often will find that the statistical techniques most appropriate for analyzing simulation data are those drawn from the analysis of variance family. The analysis of variance is most commonly used in simulations designed to probe the impacts of several independent variables upon a single dependent variable at a single point in time. That being the case, those whose statistical training is heavily regression-oriented (a category that would include, for example, virtually all

quantitatively-oriented economists, most quantitatively-oriented political scientists, and many quantitatively-oriented sociologists), with
only minimal exposure to the analysis of variance, may well have some
retooling to do before they are ready to analyze the output from their
simulation exercises. On the other hand, if the simulation focuses on
the manner in which some dependent variable changes over time, then
time-series regression techniques may well be the most appropriate
tools of statistical analysis, leaving those whose primary statistical
training is econometric rather than psychometric at a comparative
advantage.

GUARDING AGAINST SIMULATION ERRORS

In studying complex systems via computer simulation modeling
several types of error can occur (Shannon, 1975).

Design Errors

Minimizing errors in design involves, as a first step, constructing a
set of hypotheses about the manner in which the elements of the model
interact. These hypotheses are based on whatever information is avail
able, including relevant theory, prior research, observation, and the
researcher's intuition. In simulations, just as in standard empirical
analyses, design errors can be of several types (Ackoff and Sasieni
1968). The researcher may mistakenly include irrelevant variables in
the model, unduly complicating it and potentially obscuring the effect
of variables that do matter; relevant variables may be mistakenly ex
cluded from the model, undermining the generalizability of the relation
ships observed in the simulation output; the appropriate variables ma
be included in the model, but their effects may be incorrectly repre
sented (for example, by being modeled as linear when a nonlinear
specification is more appropriate); and the specification of the relation
ships between controlled and uncontrolled variables may be incorrect
again undermining generalizability.

How can design errors be minimized? A key is what has been jokingl
called the "binocular trauma test": one shows the model to as man
informed observers as possible, and if these observers report that th
model hurts them right between the eyes when they look at it, on
concludes that a problem exists. That is, if something about the mode

"just doesn't look right" to these observers, then one would do well to reconsider this aspect of the model, large or small. This obviously is a tremendously subjective approach, for there is, as the old saw has it, "no accounting for taste." Even so, it makes considerable sense to solicit advice and evaluations of a model from knowledgeable outsiders. A more systematic approach, and one we highly recommend, is to subject the model's assumptions, parameter values, and probability distributions to empirical testing whenever possible. If one can collect some data about the phenomenon under consideration, then one can greatly enhance the extent to which the simulation is rooted in the real world rather than in a wild flight of fancy.

Programming Errors

Programming errors also can occur, irrespective of whether the programming is done by the researcher who designed the model or by someone else. Obviously, however, the potential for miscommunication increases when there is a division of labor, and it increases greatly when there is a complex division of labor among several people. The potential for miscommunication increases, too, when the problem under consideration is very complex, because in that case the simulation model, reflecting the problem, is itself likely to be complex.

To work efficiently, programmers need a model that is completely specified before they begin coding. Changes in the model typically are more difficult to incorporate once programming has begun than beforehand. "Making it up as you go" is the kiss of death for programming, since the programmer must know where the program is leading; even a seemingly minor change in the model may lead to a need to begin coding all over again. It also is true that along the way programmers may have to make judgment calls or specify details that help determine whether the model performs as its designers expected. If the programmers have not previously engaged in simulation coding, the advantages of using a general-purpose user language increase, because the programmers would have to pass through a potentially problematic learning period in order to employ a special-purpose simulation language.

Predicting how long programming and debugging will take may prove difficult, especially if the simulation model has a complex logical structure. Logical structure, rather than number of lines coded or any other measure of program size, determines total programming time. A logically simple program with few branches typically is fairly easy to conceptualize, and it can readily be checked after being translated into programming code. By contrast, a logically complex program with many branches is more likely to contain logical errors, and is more difficult to check when programmed, especially if some of the branches are followed infrequently during program execution. Thus, for example, a model of a sequential eight-step process may be easy to code, while a model of a process of only four steps may be extremely challenging if it contains numerous contingency conditions, feedback loops, and the like.

Good programming habits help to minimize programming errors. One such habit, the importance of which cannot be overstated, is thoroughly documenting variables and model logic within the program itself. In a multiprogrammer environment, such documentation helps each programmer understand and coordinate coding by the other programmers. Even if only a single programmer is involved, thorough documentation is a must. Such documentation constitutes a built-in memory within the program, and can be invaluable when the programmer's own memory fails or when new programmers are later called in to modify the original model.

A second practice that minimizes programming errors is the use of modular programming and debugging. While syntax errors will be identified the first time a particular piece of the code is executed, logical programming errors often pass unnoticed. The program may be correct in the details but inappropriate in a larger sense. For example, a syntactically error-free piece of code in a simulation of interpersonal attraction may inadvertently have the *least* similar people being attracted to one another, when what the researcher really wants is to have the *most* similar people being most attracted to one another. Whenever possible, the model should be built in independent modules which, before being linked to other modules within the model, are separately tested in order to detect syntax errors and, more problematically, unreasonableness of output. When a television set breaks down, it is relatively easy to pinpoint the problem if the components of the set are modular; one swaps out one module while leaving all the other modules alone and sees whether the problem goes away. Exactly the same logic holds for programming. And modularity increases the comprehensibility of programming code, as well as increasing the likelihood of detecting logical programming errors.

A commonly used debugging technique, especially for logical errors, is to trace by hand a set of input values through the programming structure for one or more iterations. To follow this strategy, all variables that change within one model cycle, along with the initial input values, are noted. As programming code dictates that variable values be changed, the programmer records each change and new value. This procedure allows the programmer to follow the process as programmed, step by step, until a known or suspected error is uncovered. Some programming languages provide automated ways of doing the same thing, but in many cases tracing by hand may be the best way for one to get a good feel for how the model is operating.

Data Errors

Errors in the data are concerned with variable-parameter validity (Emshoff and Sisson, 1970). This type of validity focuses on whether the simulation's variables and parameters match their assumed counterparts in the real world, a consideration that takes us back to the basic issues of external validity discussed earlier in this chapter. Sensitivity testing can be used to establish a rudimentary variable-parameter validity. If varying the input values produces output values that do not correspond to observed outcomes in the real world, then variable-parameter validity is suspect. A more rigorous procedure for establishing variable-parameter validity is drawing a sample of real-world input values and parameter values, and establishing through the use of systematic statistical analysis that the model's input values and parameters are a reasonable approximation of their empirical counterparts.

Procedural Errors

Errors of procedure can occur in many different ways; in simulation as in many other pursuits, there are many more ways to do it wrong than to do it right. Components of the model may be inappropriately linked, causing distortion in overall system performance. An inappropriate period may be selected for each cycle or iteration, so that too little or too much variance occurs within a cycle. In a dynamic model, the researcher may not allow the model to run for a sufficient number of iterations, obscuring long-term trends. If intermediate model outputs are not developed for each iteration, the researcher may be unaware that an underlying cyclical process is being obscured. Spurious relationships can appear to be real, if numerous input values are modified simultaneously.

Interpretative Errors

In addition to the errors in interpretation that can result from improper use of the model, errors can occur from using the wrong statistical procedures to analyze simulation output, or from using the appropriate procedures inappropriately. In statistical analysis, a little knowledge can be very dangerous if it conveys a false sense of mastery. Although one does not necessarily have to have a highly sophisticated command of statistical techniques in order to analyze simulation data, a strong conceptual grasp of statistics and a good working knowledge of a wide array of techniques can save one from making analytic choices that are suboptimal or simply incorrect.

CONCLUSION

Just as Charles Dickens, in *A Tale of Two Cities,* described an earlier era as "the best of times and the worst of times," computer simulation is the best of research methods and the worst of research methods. It is the best of research methods because it permits the researcher to build and test his or her own custom-made, problem-specific model, and the building and testing processes are intellectually challenging, technically demanding, flexible, scientific, and creative. It is the worst of research techniques for precisely the same reasons: The researcher must build and test his or her own custom-made, problem-specific model, and the building processes are intellectually challenging, technically demanding, flexible, scientific, and creative.

How do you go about building and running a simulation model, especially if you have never built one before? Unlike other, more standardized and routinized, research approaches, each model is different and takes on a life of its own. Nonetheless, there are several steps through which you must pass:

(1) *First, identify the dependent variable.* Just as in any other research project, the dependent variable is the phenomenon of primary interest that you want to describe, predict, and explain. Once the dependent variable has been identified, you must figure out a range for it—decide how it varies on some metric scale or according to certain categories.

(2) *Next, identify the independent variables* from prior research and your own knowledge and intuitions concerning the substance of the

model. Identify metrics or categories for the independent variables, just as for the dependent variable.

(3) *Identify some rules (algorithms) by which independent variables are translated into or affect the dependent variable.*

(4) *Decide whether some level of the independent variables* always *results in a certain consequence for the dependent variable or* usually *or* sometimes *does so.* If the former is true, use a deterministic model. If the latter is true, use a stochastic model.

(5) *Decide what to hold constant in the model while the experimental factors vary.* These constant factors become the parameters of the model. Decide at what level you are going to set each parameter, as specificity is required.

(6) *Identify the crucial aspects of human or institutional behavior that are implied by your model.* These are the assumptions underlying the model. State them explicitly.

(7) *Decide whether you are modeling a process that takes place* over time, *or decision making* at a particular point in time. If the former is true, you need to construct a dynamic model. If the latter is true, you need to construct a static model.

(8) *Develop a schematic flowchart,* either on paper or in your head, of how the model will operate. First you will generate a value for the first independent variable. If this variable takes on a certain value, it will have certain effects on other variables in the model; if it takes on a different value, it will have other effects. Then you will generate a value for the next independent variable. Given the value of the first independent variable, if the second variable takes on a certain value, it will have certain effects on other variables in the model; if it takes on a different value, it will have other effects. You continue in this vein until you have exhausted the stock of variables.

(9) *Program the steps you have just identified in the flowchart.* For this step you need programming skills that may take considerable time to acquire.

(10) *Feed input values into the model and analyze the results.* The purpose of the analysis is to probe the linkage between the independent variables, on the one hand, and the dependent variable, on the other, just as in standard empirical research. If the model is at all complex, you will probably need to analyze the results statistically.

This concludes our initial overview of computer simulation modeling. To this point, we have treated computer simulation models in the abstract. We believe that the best way for novices to learn modeling strategies and tactics is for them to develop and run a computer simulation model of some problem of interest. Before striking out on their own, however, beginners would profit from considering, in depth, some concrete social science applications of these strategies and tactics. Accordingly, in the next three chapters, we provide a series of illustrations of computer simulation modeling as applied to particular problems in social science.

5

Simulation #1—An Exercise in Theory Building

In this chapter we describe a simulation model we developed explicitly for purposes of theory building.

THE PROBLEM

During the last two decades, scholarly research on public budgeting has focused mainly on incremental annual changes in line items, the most specific component of any budget request. After the *line item,* the *program* constitutes the second lowest level of budgetary decision making. Political scientists distinguish between redistributive and non-redistributive programs. Redistributive programs reallocate scarce resources from one social group or class to another—normally, though not invariably, from "haves" to "have-nots." Since redistributive decisions by their very nature are conflictual, as a conflict-avoidance strategy, policy debate tends to focus on the lower level of yearly changes in line items rather than on programmatic considerations per se.

The third level of budgetary decision making involves *functions* rather than programs or line items. Here we reduce the wide array of functional areas in which the federal government operates to defense versus nondefense spending.

At the fourth and highest level of budgetary decision making, attention focuses on the appropriate *size of the public sector.* If the budgetary process begins on this level, determination of the aggregate level of government spending provides the context within which all subsequent decision making operates. On the other hand, if this question is not directly confronted, the size of the budget ends up being determined by the aggregation of less inclusive lower-level decisions.

When we distinguish among the line item, program, function, and aggregate levels of budgetary decision making, we do not assume that explicit budgetary decisions are necessarily made at all four levels, or in any fixed order. However, these four types of decision *are* made in any budgetary process, if only by default. *The purpose of this analysis is to shed light on how the order in which these decisions are made affects spending levels and priorities.*

The basic argument is that the sequencing of these four decisions can significantly affect budgetary outcomes. At the lowest, most detailed level of decision making, the only overt issue is whether somewhat more, the same amount, or somewhat less will be spent this year than was spent last year on a particular line item. Such decision making obviously is too narrow to address directly the issues upon which attention would naturally focus in higher level decision making—issues related to programmatic or functional emphases and the total size of the public sector. If budgetary decision making begins at the line-item level, however, a complete set of such decisions implicitly determines every higher level budgetary decision. Aggregating line items determines how much redistributive spending will be budgeted, how large the defense component of the budget will be relative to the nondefense component, and ultimately how large the public sector will be.

Redistributive decisions are explicitly made at the program or statute level. Starting the decision-making process at this level (which we term a "mixed" decision sequence, since it begins at a middle level in the four-tiered decision hierarchy) does not preclude subsequent decision making at the line-item level, but a complete set of program-level decisions does implicitly determine, by aggregation, how spending will be distributed across functions and how large the government budget will be.

Questions of how large or small defense spending will be relative to nondefense spending are explicitly addressed at the function or policy level. Starting the decision-making process at this level constrains rather than precludes explicit decision making at the program and line-item levels, but it implicitly determines the size of the public sector. Accordingly, this middle-down movement constitutes a second type of mixed decision sequence.

The top-down decision sequence begins with a consideration of macroeconomic fiscal concerns, but leaves open the possibility of explicit, albeit constrained, decision making at each of the three lower levels. Given such a top-down approach, debate over the size of the public sector and of the total budget can overtly occur in the initial phase of the congressional budget cycle and can affect lower level budgetary decisions later in the cycle.

THE MODEL

We develop a computer simulation model in order to clarify the budgetary consequences of the bottom-up and top-down decision sequences. In order to keep the simulation manageable, this exercise focuses exclusively on the two polar types of decision sequence, ignoring mixed sequences, though we do complicate matters by probing the impact of these two sequences under a range of different conditions. These conditions involve, first, Congress's general *allocation strategy*. Under an existing base strategy, programs or functions are treated in proportion to their share of the existing budget, while under a targeted strategy, certain programs or functions are singled out for special treatment. Also taken into account are the *national economic climate*, represented in the model by alternative specifications for rapid growth, slow growth, or economic cutbacks, and the prevailing *congressional orientation toward growth*—liberal, moderate, or conservative.

The model is deterministic, in that it combines the four independent variables (the two budget sequences, the two budget strategies, the three economic conditions, and the three congressional orientations) in every way possible, producing a total of 36 different budgetary outcomes. These outcomes are represented by five separate variables: *total federal spending; total defense spending; total nondefense spending; total redistributive spending; and total nonredistributive spending.* The model runs for ten years, at the end of which we gauge the budgetary impact of bottom-up versus top-down decision sequencing under the various simulated conditions.

In starting the simulation, we specify total first-year federal spending of a trillion dollars, roughly the size of the current federal budget. This budget is partitioned, also in a manner approximating the current budget, into redistributive and nonredistributive programs ($400 billion and $600 billion, respectively); defense and nondefense functions ($300 billion and $700 billion, respectively); and nondefense-nonredistributive and other spending ($300 billion and $700 billion, respectively).

With these start-up values fixed, the percentage by which Congress is willing to increase or decrease federal spending is determined. This determination is based on the nation's economic condition and on the dominant political orientation in Congress. Here we present the underlying logic of this determination in contingency table format, which permits us to say, in effect, "If X is true and if Y is true, then Z is the consequence." We employ a contingency table (see Table 5.1) rather than the more traditional flowchart because we are dealing in this simulation with a relatively simple combination of circumstances. In more complex budgetary simulations, we have used flowcharting techniques to represent the underlying process; one such flowchart of a portion of the budgetary process (the consideration of the budget proposal in one chamber of Congress) is shown in Figure 5.1. Beginning in the upper left-hand corner of the flowchart, one can trace the consideration of the budget proposal from start to finish by following any sequence of "yes" or "no" arrows through to ultimate passage or rejection. In reality, such a flowchart is simply a large, multidimensional contingency table, since all it does is pose and answer a series of "if-then" questions.

Returning to Table 5.1, we see that in all instances, the slower the economic growth rate, the smaller the percentage by which total spending increases or the larger the percentage by which it decreases. Similarly, for any given economic condition the more liberal the orientation of Congress, the greater the percentage increase or the smaller the percentage decrease. Thus, for example, under conditions of rapid economic growth a liberal Congress increases the budget by 15% per year, while in an economic cutback situation a conservative Congress imposes a 10% yearly cut. In addition, the size of the yearly increment or decrement varies as a function of the congressional decision sequence. When Congress makes budgetary decisions from the top down, the national economic condition and the ideological orientation that prevails in Congress alone determine the size of the increment or decrement. When Congress makes budgetary decisions from the bottom up, however, pressures to support constituent-oriented programs are so great that in the absence of an overall budget goal, spending climbs to a higher level than it would otherwise attain; in the model, spending is increased by 3% over its level in the corresponding top-down sequence.

After the size of the total yearly increment has been set, programmatic and functional allocations must be determined. Under the existing base allocation strategy, all budgetary categories (defense and nondefense, redistribution and nonredistribution) are first increased in proportion to their share of the existing budget. Then this proportional increase is supplemented, for a favored spending area (nondefense or redistribution for a liberal Congress, defense or nonredistribution for a conservative Congress), by the percentage at which the overall budget is growing, as shown in Table 5.1, with the difference being subtracted from spending on the pertinent nonfavored area. Thus, in good times,

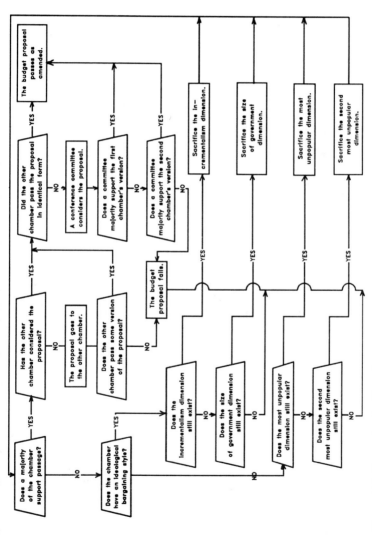

Figure 5.1. Example of a Flowchart

83

Table 5.1

Yearly Percentage Change in Total Spending as a Function of
Congressional Orientation and National Economic Conditions

Economic Condition	Orientation of Congress		
	Conservative	Moderate	Liberal
Rapid growth	.05	.10	.15
Slow growth	.03	.06	.09
Cutback	−.10	−.05	.00

when the total budget is expanding, Congress devotes an even larger
share of new spending to supporting favored programs and functions,
secure in the knowledge that increases are still available for the maintenance of what it deems less critical programs or functions. In tighter
economic circumstances, Congress behaves more cautiously, sticking
closer to the existing base.

Under the targeted allocation strategy, Congress begins by reserving
two thirds of the total yearly increase for its favorite types of spending.
It then increases this percentage at the rate of the overall budgetary
increase, again as shown in Table 5.1. Thus, for example, under conditions of rapid economic growth a liberal Congress allocates 81% of the
total increment (the general 66% target plus 15% from the matrix in
Table 5.1) to redistributive programs, and only 19% to nonredistributive
programs; in a slow growth period the same Congress allocates 75% of
the increment to redistributive programs, while in a cutback period the
liberal Congress has no increment to allocate. A conservative Congress
mirrors this general strategy, allocating 71% of the increment to nonredistributive programs under rapid growth (the targeted 66% plus the
5% associated with rapid growth) and 69% under slow growth; during
economic cutbacks, the conservative Congress exacts 76% of the yearly
decrement (a targeted 66% plus the 10% from the Table 5.1 matrix) from
redistributive programs and nondefense functions. A moderate Congress begins by allocating 50% of the yearly increment or decrement to
each type of program or function, and then, like a conservative or liberal
Congress, modifies these targets as a function of the size of the overall
increment.

Finally, the bottom-up decision-making sequence begins with the
determination of the yearly increment, with a 3% add-on to reflect
congressional responsiveness to constituent pressures. Decision making is complete at this point, with no explicit attention paid to functional

or programmatic allocations. Still, spending levels are calculable for the various functional and programmatic categories. Under the top-down sequence, decisions at each level are made before decision making at the next lower level is initiated. Hence, the size of the overall budget is set first; the defense and nondefense budgets are set next, thereby constraining the relative amounts available for redistributive and nonredistributive programs; and finally, allocations of the increments still available for redistributive and nonredistributive allocations are made.

This rendition of the process by which one chamber of Congress considers a budget proposal was translated into concrete terms in the form of a program written in BASIC (see Table 5.2). It is well beyond our purpose here to teach BASIC programming, but we would encourage novices to scan the program, bearing in mind our verbal formulation of the process, to see whether they can successfully match aspects of the former with aspects of the latter.

RESULTS

Table 5.3 presents the first set of simulation results, which pertain to the total size of the federal budget. Looking down the table, we see that over the simulated 10-year period the condition of the national economy has a pronounced impact on total spending, which varies by as much as 15% per year under differing national economic conditions. Compounded over a 10-year period, these yearly differentials yield total spending figures that are more than twice as large during a decade of rapid economic growth as they are during sustained economic cutbacks. The same is true of the impact of congressional orientations. Depending on national economic conditions, over the 10-year period a more liberal Congress may spend almost twice as much as a more conservative one.

Table 5.3 also indicates that whether Congress employs an existing base or a targeted allocation strategy has absolutely no bearing on total spending. This is simply because decisions about how to allocate the budgetary increment or decrement are made within the context of an increment or decrement of a given size. More to the point of the simulation, we see in Table 5.3 that a decade of adhering to a bottom-up strategy can lead to total spending differences of hundreds of billions of dollars. In a top-down sequence, total spending is determined solely by the interaction of congressional orientations and economic conditions.

Table 5.2
Listing of the BASIC Model

```
10  REM BUDGET:
20  REM Budget Hierarchy and Sequencing
30  OPEN "o",#1,"bdata"
40  DIM ECCG(3,3)
50  REM  ECCG has economic condition in rows: 1 = rapid growth;
60  REM     2 = slow growth; 3 = cutback;
70  REM  ECCG has congressional orientation toward growth in columns;
80  REM     1 = conservative; 2 = moderate; 3 = liberal;
90  REM BUD = 1 = bottom up strategy;  = 2 = top down
100 REM total number of cases = 3 x 3 x 2 = 18
110    ECCG(1,1) = .05            'rapid growth, lib co on bud growth'
120    ECCG(1,2) = .1             'rapid growth, mod co on budg growth'
130    ECCG(1,3) = .15            'rapid growth; lib co on budg growth'
140    ECCG(2,1) = .03            'slow growth; cons co on budg growth'
150    ECCG(2,2) = .06            'slow growth; mod co on budg growth'
160    ECCG(2,3) = .09            'slow growth; lib co on budg growth'
170    ECCG(3,1) = -.1            'conservative, cutback'
180    ECCG(3,2) = -.05           'moderate, cutback'
190    ECCG(3,3) = 0              'liberal, cutback'
200    FOR EC  = 1 TO 3           'varies economic conditions'
210    FOR CG  = 1 TO 3           'varies congressional orientation'
220    X = 0
230 IF ECCG(EC,CG)< 0 THEN X = 1
240 IF ECCG(EC,CG)< 0 THEN ECCG(EC,CG) = ABS(ECCG(EC,CG))
250    FOR BUD = 1 TO 2           'varies budget strategy'
260    TBUD = 1000                'total budget, in billions'
270    REDIS = 400                'redistributive spending'
280    NONRED = 600               'non-redistributive spending'
290    NONDR = 300                'non-defense, non-redis'
300    DEFN = 300                 'defense spending'
310    NONDEF  = 700              'non-defense spending'
320    TBUDI = 0                  'total budget increase'
330    REDISI = 0                 'redistributive increase - total'
340    NONREDI = 0                'non-redistributive increase - total'
350    NONDRI = 0                 'non-defense, non-redis increase -total'
360    DEFI = 0                   'defense spending increase - total'
370    NONDEFI = 0                'non-defense increase - total'
380    FOR YEAR = 1 TO 10
390    IF BUD = 2 THEN 690
400 IF X = 0 THEN INCRE = ABS(TBUD * (ECCG(EC,CG) + .03))
410 IF X = 1 THEN INCRE = ABS(TBUD * (-ECCG(EC,CG) + .03))
420    REM y on variable means increase for the budget year
430 IF CG=1 THEN 490
440 IF CG=2 THEN 530
450    IF X = 0 THEN REDISY = ((REDIS/TBUD) + ECCG(EC,CG)) * INCRE
451 IF X=0 THEN NONREDY = INCRE - REDISY
460 IF X =1 THEN NONREDIS = ((NONREDIS/TBUD) - ECCG(EC,CG)) * INCRE
470 IF X=1 THEN REDISY = INCRE - REDISY
480 GOTO 570
490 IF X=0 THEN NONREDY = ((NONRED/TBUD) - ECCG(EC,CG)) * INCRE
```

(continued)

Table 5.2 (Continued)

```
495 IF X=0 THEN REDISY = INCRE - NONREDY
500 IF X=1 THEN REDISY = ((REDIS/TBUD) - ECCG(EC,CG)) * INCRE
510 IF X=1 THEN NONREDY = INCRE - REDISY
520 GOTO 550
530 NONREDY = (.5 * INCRE)
540 REDISY = .5 * INCRE
550 IF CG=1 THEN GOTO 610
560 IF CG=2 THEN GOTO 650
570  IF X=0 THEN NONDRY = ((NONDR/NONRED) + ECCG(EC,CG)) * NONREDY
575  IF X=0 THEN DEFY= NONREDY - NONDRY
580 IF X=1 THEN DEFY = ((DEF/NONRED)- ECCG(EC,CG)) * NONREDY
581 IF X=1 THEN NONDRY = NONREDY - DEFY
590  NONDEFY = REDISY + NONDRY
600 GOTO 680
610 IF X=0 THEN DEFY = ((DEFN/NONRED) + ECCG(EC,CG)) * NONREDY
625 IF X=0 THEN NONDEFY = INCRE - DEFY
630 IF X=0 THEN NONDRY = INCRE - (REDISY + DEFY)
631 IF X=1 THEN NONDEFY = ((NONDEF/NONRED) + ECCG(EC,CG)) * NONREDY
632 IF X=1 THEN DEFY = INCRE - NONDEFY
633 IF X=1 THEN NONDRY = INCRE - (REDISY + DEFY)
640 GOTO 680
650 NONDRY = NONREDISY * .5
660 DEFY = NONREDISY * .5
670 NONDEFY = INCRE - DEFY
680 GOTO 920
690   INCRE = ABS(TBUD * ECCG(EC,CG))
700   IF ECCG(EC,CG)< 0 THEN X = 1 AND ECCG(EC,CG) = ABS(ECCG(EC,CG))
710 IF CG=1 THEN 830
720 IF CG=2 THEN 911
730  IF X=0 THEN NONDEFY = ((NONDEF/TBUD) + ECCG(EC,CG)) * INCRE
740  IF X=0 THEN DEFY = INCRE - NONDEFY
750  IF X=1 THEN DEFY = ((DEFN/TBUD)- ECCG(EC,CG)) *INCRE
760  IF X = 1 THEN NONDEFY = INCRE - DEFY
770  IF X=0 THEN REDISY = ((REDIS/NONDEF) + ECCG(EC,CG)) * NONDEFY
780 IF X=0 THEN NONREDY = INCRE - REDISY
790 IF X=1 THEN NONREDY = ((NONRED/NONDEF) - ECCG(EC,CG)) * NONDEFY
800 IF X=1 THEN REDISY = INCRE - NONREDY
810   NONDRY = NONDEFY - REDISY
820 GOTO 920
830 IF X=0 THEN DEFY = ((DEFN/TBUD) + ECCG(EC,CG)) * INCRE
840 IF X=0 THEN NONDEFY = INCRE - DEFY
850 IF X=1 THEN NONDEFY = ((NONDEF/TBUD) - ECCG(EC,CG)) * INCRE
860 IF X=1 THEN DEFY = INCRE - NONDEFY
870 IF X=0 THEN NONREDY = ((NONRED/NONDEF) + ECCG(EC,CG)) * NONDEFY
880 IF X=0 THEN REDISY = INCRE - REDISY
890 IF X=1 THEN REDISY = ((REDIS/NONDEF) - ECCG(EC,CG)) * NONDEFY
900 IF X=1 THEN NONREDISY = INCRE - REDISY
910 NONDRY = NONDEFY - REDISY:GOTO 920
911 DEFY = .5 * INCRE
912 NONDEFY = INCRE - DEFY
913 REDISY = .5 * NONDEFY
914 NONREDY = INCRE - REDISY
915 NONDRY = INCRE - (DEFY + REDISY)
```

(continued)

Table 5.2 (Continued)

```
920    IF X = 1 THEN TBUD = TBUD - INCRE
930    IF X = 0 THEN TBUD = TBUD + INCRE
940    TBUDI = TBUDI + TBUD
950    IF X = 1 THEN   NONDEF = NONDEF - NONDEFY
960    IF X = 0 THEN   NONDEF = NONDEF + NONDEFY
970    NONDEFI = NONDEFI + NONDEF
980    IF X = 1 THEN DEFN = DEFN - DEFY
990    IF X = 0 THEN DEFN = DEFN + DEFY
1000   DEFI = DEFI + DEFN
1010   IF X = 1 THEN REDIS = REDIS - REDISY
1020   IF X = 0 THEN REDIS = REDIS + REDISY
1030   REDISI = REDISI + REDIS
1040   IF X = 1 THEN NONRED = NONRED - NONREDY
1050   IF X = 0 THEN NONRED = NONRED + NONREDY
1060   NONREDI = NONREDI + NONRED
1070   IF X = 1 THEN NONDR = NONDR - NONDRY
1080   IF X = 0 THEN NONDR = NONDR + NONDRY
1090   NONDRI = NONDRI + NONDR
1100   NEXT YEAR
1110   F1$=" # # # ######### ######## ######## ######## ######## ########"
1120   PRINT#1,USING F1$;EC;CG;BUD;TBUDI;NONDEFI;DEFI;REDISI;NONREDI;NONDRI
1130   NEXT BUD
1140   NEXT CG
1150   NEXT EC
1160   CLOSE#1
1170   END
```

Thus, for example, under cutback conditions a liberal Congress simply replicates the original trillion dollar budget each year, producing a 10-year spending total of $10 trillion. In the bottom-up case, however, constituency pressures add 3% to each annual budget, and over a 10-year period these increments compound to the extent that, for example, the $10 trillion top-down spending total for a liberal Congress under cutback conditions grows to more than $11.8 trillion when bottom-up decision making is in force.

The simulated 10-year spending totals for defense and nondefense functions are shown in Tables 5.4 and 5.5. A liberal Congress spends relatively less on defense than a conservative Congress does, and redistributive spending during a rapid growth period surpasses that in slow growth and cutback periods—outcomes that directly reflect two of the key assumptions in the model. It is less immediately apparent, and therefore more interesting, that decision sequencing has complex interactive effects on defense and nondefense spending. One of these interactive effects warrants special scrutiny.

This interactive effect can be glimpsed in the portions of Table 5.3 that focus on nondefense allocations by a liberal or moderate Congress under rapid economic growth. Over 10 years, as long as Congress

Table 5.3
Ten-Year Totals in Federal Spending (in Billions)

Rapid Growth

Congressional Orientation

	Conservative Strategy		*Moderate Strategy*		*Liberal Strategy*	
	Base	*Targeted*	*Base*	*Targeted*	*Base*	*Targeted*
Bottom-up	15645	15645	20814	20814	27755	27755
Top-down	13207	13207	17531	17531	23349	23349

Slow Growth

Congressional Orientation

	Conservative Strategy		*Moderate Strategy*		*Liberal Strategy*	
	Base	*Targeted*	*Base*	*Targeted*	*Base*	*Targeted*
Bottom-up	13972	13972	16560	16560	19655	19655
Top-down	11808	11808	13972	13972	16560	16560

Cutback

Congressional Orientation

	Conservative Strategy		*Moderate Strategy*		*Liberal Strategy*	
	Base	*Targeted*	*Base*	*Targeted*	*Base*	*Targeted*
Bottom-up	6856	6856	8963	8963	11808	11808
Top-down	5862	5862	7624	7624	10000	10000

employs a targeted allocation strategy the bottom-up decision sequence produces greater nondefense spending than does the top-down sequence. Indeed, this is the general result in Table 5.5, because *total* spending is higher in the bottom-up case, nondefense spending—which accounts for the majority of the budget—is higher, too.

There are two conspicuous exceptions to this pattern: for a moderate or liberal Congress during a rapid growth period, bottom-up decision making actually depresses the nondefense budget under an existing base allocation strategy. The explanation, which is most readily grasped

Table 5.4
Ten-Year Totals in Defense Spending (in Billions)

Rapid Growth

Congressional Orientation

	Conservative Strategy		*Moderate Strategy*		*Liberal Strategy*	
	Base	*Targeted*	*Base*	*Targeted*	*Base*	*Targeted*
Bottom-up	5387	6091	7801	7332	8990	6365
Top-down	4148	5277	4259	6012	3982	5536

Slow Growth

Congressional Orientation

	Conservative Strategy		*Moderate Strategy*		*Liberal Strategy*	
	Base	*Targeted*	*Base*	*Targeted*	*Base*	*Targeted*
Bottom-up	4527	5059	4231	4103	4432	3467
Top-down	3602	4247	3908	4748	4205	4640

Cutback

Congressional Orientation

	Conservative Strategy		*Moderate Strategy*		*Liberal Strategy*	
	Base	*Targeted*	*Base*	*Targeted*	*Base*	*Targeted*
Bottom-up	2244	2771	2667	2720	3479	3174
Top-down	2061	2007	2185	1693	3000	7000

in the case of the liberal Congress, is that the start-up value for non-defense spending is 70% of the total budget. According to the existing base allocation strategy, this translates into a 70% allocation of the increment to nondefense functions, supplemented during rapid growth by an extra 15% because of the liberal Congress's enthusiasm for nondefense spending. Thus 85% of the total increment is available for nondefense functions, to which it is allocated under top-down decision making. By contrast, under the targeted growth strategy, a liberal Congress begins by reserving 66% of the total increment for

Table 5.5
Ten-Year Totals in Nondefense Spending (in Billions)

Rapid Growth

Congressional Orientation

	Conservative Strategy		Moderate Strategy		Liberal Strategy	
	Base	*Targeted*	*Base*	*Targeted*	*Base*	*Targeted*
Bottom-up	10258	9554	13013	13482	18765	21390
Top-down	9059	7930	13272	11519	19367	17813

Slow Growth

Congressional Orientation

	Conservative Strategy		Moderate Strategy		Liberal Strategy	
	Base	*Targeted*	*Base*	*Targeted*	*Base*	*Targeted*
Bottom-up	9445	8913	12329	12458	15222	16187
Top-down	8205	7560	10064	9224	12355	11920

Cutback

Congressional Orientation

	Conservative Strategy		Moderate Strategy		Liberal Strategy	
	Base	*Targeted*	*Base*	*Targeted*	*Base*	*Targeted*
Bottom-up	4612	4085	6296	6244	8329	8634
Top-down	3801	3855	5439	5931	7000	7000

nondefense functions—less than the 70% reserved under the existing base strategy; then, given rapid growth, the liberal Congress adds another 15%. This targeted nondefense allocation is large, but not as large as the allocation that results from bottom-up decision making, since in the bottom-up case the total increment is larger, by a factor of 3% compounded annually.

The same patterns hold for the redistributive and nonredistributive allocations, which are shown in Tables 5.6 and 5.7. Once again, large-scale spending differences emerge as a function of national economic

Table 5.6
Ten-Year Totals in Redistributive Spending (in Billions)

Rapid Growth

Congressional Orientation

	Conservative Strategy		Moderate Strategy		Liberal Strategy	
	Base	*Targeted*	*Base*	*Targeted*	*Base*	*Targeted*
Bottom-up	5690	5468	10344	10813	16289	18914
Top-down	5059	4270	8447	6711	14070	12758

Slow Growth

Congressional Orientation

	Conservative Strategy		Moderate Strategy		Liberal Strategy	
	Base	*Targeted*	*Base*	*Targeted*	*Base*	*Targeted*
Bottom-up	5305	5112	7387	7871	9483	11531
Top-down	4650	4174	5973	5246	7702	7690

Cutback

Congressional Orientation

	Conservative Strategy		Moderate Strategy		Liberal Strategy	
	Base	*Targeted*	*Base*	*Targeted*	*Base*	*Targeted*
Bottom-up	2565	1681	3605	3502	4782	5247
Top-down	1949	1610	3030	2212	4000	4000

conditions and congressional orientation; since redistributive issues lie at the heart of the distinction between liberalism and conservatism, the absence of pronounced liberal-conservative spending differences on redistributive programs simply would not be a credible result. More significantly, comparing each pair of bottom-up and top-down spending totals in Table 5.6 reveals that in every case the amount allocated to redistributive programs under a bottom-up sequence exceeds the amount allocated under a top-down sequence.

Table 5.7
Ten-Year Totals in Nonredistributive Spending (in Billions)

Rapid Growth

Congressional Orientation

	Conservative Strategy		Moderate Strategy		Liberal Strategy	
	Base	*Targeted*	*Base*	*Targeted*	*Base*	*Targeted*
Bottom-up	9956	10178	10470	10001	11466	8841
Top-down	8148	8937	9084	10820	9279	10591

Slow Growth

Congressional Orientation

	Conservative Strategy		Moderate Strategy		Liberal Strategy	
	Base	*Targeted*	*Base*	*Targeted*	*Base*	*Targeted*
Bottom-up	8667	8860	9173	8690	10172	8124
Top-down	7158	7634	7999	8726	8858	8870

Cutback

Congressional Orientation

	Conservative Strategy		Moderate Strategy		Liberal Strategy	
	Base	*Targeted*	*Base*	*Targeted*	*Base*	*Targeted*
Bottom-up	4291	5148	5359	5461	7025	6560
Top-down	3913	4252	4594	5412	6000	6000

Why are there no exceptions? The answer is that the start-up value for redistributive spending is 60% of the total budget, rather than the 70% devoted to nondefense spending. A closer look at Table 5.6 also reveals that the magnitude of the bottom-up versus top-down spending differences varies enormously from condition to condition. To cite only the two extreme cases: for a liberal Congress that employs a targeted allocation strategy under conditions of rapid economic growth, bottom-up redistributive spending is almost half again as large as top-down redistributive spending; however, for a conservative Congress that

employs a targeted allocation strategy during an economic cutback
total bottom-up spending on redistributive programs outruns total top-
down spending by only about 4%. More generally, as attention shifts
from the top to the bottom of the table, and from the right to the left
the spending differential attributable to decision sequencing drops off

CONCLUSION

The underlying message of these results is that the sequence in which
budgetary decision making occurs has potentially important effects on
budget outcomes. To be sure, these effects pale alongside those of
national economic conditions and prevailing congressional orientations. Nor are these effects always straightforward. The simulation
results reveal that the direction and magnitude of these effects vary
markedly from one set of conditions to another. Accordingly, our result
suggest that decision sequencing should be incorporated into budgetary
theory on a contingency basis, with full account taken of the circumstances under which sequencing affects budget outcomes in various
ways.

6

Simulation #2—An Exercise in Policy Analysis

The simulation model described in Chapter 5 addressed a theoretical issue of concern to social scientists interested in the budgetary process. In this chapter we describe a simulation model that differs from the one developed in the last chapter in many respects, the most fundamental being the purpose for which it is intended: the model described here was developed explicitly for purposes of analyzing potential avenues of policy response to the spread of acquired immunodeficiency syndrome (AIDS).

This application exercise develops a computer simulation model of the sexual transmission of AIDS for homosexual males, bisexual males, heterosexual males, and heterosexual females. We have previously referred to flowcharts and contingency tables as the backbone of a computer simulation model, but here our attention centers on prediction equations for the number of new sexually transmitted AIDS cases per category per year. These prediction equations motivate a simulation model in which the independent variables are, for each of the four focal categories, the transmission rate per act of intercourse, the frequency of intercourse per month, the average number of relationships per month, and the initial incidence of infection. The values of the first three of these variables are varied in the simulation to represent the leverage that various policy alternatives could potentially provide toward slowing the spread of AIDS. The simulation is thus designed to address some policy dimensions of one of the most dramatic new sociomedical developments of this century.

THE PROBLEM

The commonly accepted explanation of how AIDS is transmitted is exposure to the internal body fluids of an infected person—primarily blood and semen. The three major high-risk populations in the United States have been homosexual males having anal intercourse with infected persons (exposure to semen); intravenous drug users sharing needles with other infected users (exposure to blood); and recipients of AIDS-infected blood transfusions (exposure to blood).

Originally confined to these three populations in the United States, AIDS is now found in other groups as well. Through bisexuals, who have sex with both men and women, as well as through sexually active heterosexual male drug users, AIDS has begun to be sexually transmitted to the heterosexual population. Thus heterosexual intercourse has become an additional means of transmitting AIDS, although heterosexual contact still accounts for a small proportion of total AIDS cases in the United States.

Handicapping the empirical study of AIDS dissemination is the fact that sexual behavior is an extremely sensitive topic not subject to great scientific rigor, especially when homosexual and bisexual behavior are the topics of analysis. No comprehensive study of American sexual mores has been conducted for almost four decades, and no reliable current statistics are available on the numbers of either homosexual or bisexual men. Yet the size of the bisexual population in particular is key to estimating the sexual transmission of AIDS from the homosexual to the heterosexual population.

From a policy perspective, the issue is simple. How can the human devastation wrought by AIDS be minimized? The most straightforward solution is equally simple: find a medical preventive or cure, paralleling the Salk polio vaccine of the 1950s. Millions and millions of dollars currently are being spent in an attempt to do exactly that. In the absence of a medical preventive or cure for AIDS, however, where does it make the most sense to attack the disease? If the ill effects of sexual behavior cannot be overcome medically, then it makes sense to encourage people to modify their sexual behavior (and, of course, to curtail the sharing of needles) in ways that could minimize the spread of the disease. The following have all been suggested as means of slowing down the spread of AIDS:

- Encourage sexually monogamous relationships, thereby reducing the number of sexual partners with whom people come in contact.
- Encourage sexual restraint, thereby reducing the number of acts of intercourse in which people engage.
- Encourage AIDS testing, thereby alerting people that they are infected with the AIDS virus and lowering the frequency of sexual contact between infected and noninfected people.

- Encourage the use of condoms and other physical protection, thereby lowering the rate at which AIDS is sexually transmitted.

Which of these suggestions hold out the greatest potential for combating the spread of AIDS? When we ask this question, we are asking about the effects of courses of action that have not been undertaken. Because the analysis is being conducted prior to the adoption of any policy that would lead people to modify their sexual behavior, we cannot assess these impacts empirically. Rather, we must do our best to imagine what these impacts might be. To use our imaginations in a systematic way, we undertake a computer simulation.

The utility of the simulation approach in this case stems directly from the nature of the question of interest. If we were interested solely in predicting how many AIDS victims there would be in some future year, there would be no reason for us to construct a computer simulation model; the Center for Disease Control's projections, based on some fairly simple curve-fitting, approximate the actual spread of the disease reasonably well. But what we are undertaking is, in effect, sensitivity testing designed to probe the potential impacts of various means of slowing the spread of AIDS and, for this purpose, the simulation approach is extremely well suited.

THE MODEL

When we consider the sexual transmission of AIDS, four populations are of interest: homosexual or "gay" men (M_G); bisexual men (M_B); heterosexual or "straight" men (M_S); and heterosexual or "straight" women (F_S). Gay and bisexual women have been excluded from consideration.

Among members of the four focal populations, five types of relationships potentially involve sexual intercourse (see Table 6.1). With the advent of AIDS, all four populations can be subdivided into two groups, each composed of those who are infected (I) with the AIDS virus and those who are not (N). The members of these eight groups can then engage in 18 types of sexual pairing (see Table 6.2).

The last column in Table 6.2 indicates whether it is possible for AIDS to be transmitted in a given type of sexual pairing. Obviously, when neither partner is infected, there is no possibility of transmission. Nor can the AIDS virus be transmitted when both partners already have been

Table 6.1

Types of Sexual Pairings Among Members of the Four Populations

$$(1)\ M_G \times M_G$$
$$(2)\ M_G \times M_B$$
$$(3)\ M_B \times M_B$$
$$(4)\ M_B \times F_S$$
$$(5)\ M_S \times F_S$$

NOTE: M_G = homosexual (gay) male; M_B = bisexual male; M_S = heterosexual (straight) male; F_S = heterosexual (straight) female.

Table 6.2

Types of Sexual Pairings in the AIDS Era

Intercourse Type		Number Infected	Possible to Transmit AIDS?
(1)	$IM_G \times IM_G$	2	no
(2)	$IM_G \times NM_G$	1	yes
(3)	$NM_G \times NM_G$	0	no
(4)	$IM_G \times IM_B$	2	no
(5)	$IM_G \times NM_B$	1	yes
(6)	$NM_G \times IM_B$	1	yes
(7)	$NM_G \times NM_B$	0	no
(8)	$IM_B \times IM_B$	2	no
(9)	$IM_B \times NM_B$	1	yes
(10)	$NM_B \times NM_B$	0	no
(11)	$IM_B \times IF_S$	2	no
(12)	$IM_B \times NF_S$	1	yes
(13)	$NM_B \times IF_S$	1	yes
(14)	$NM_B \times NF_S$	0	no
(15)	$IM_S \times IF_S$	2	no
(16)	$IM_S \times NF_S$	1	yes
(17)	$NM_S \times IF_S$	1	yes
(18)	$NM_S \times NF_S$	0	no

NOTE: IM_G = infected gay man
NM_G = noninfected gay man
IM_B = infected bisexual man
NM_B = noninfected bisexual man
IM_S = infected straight man
NM_S = noninfected straight man
IF_S = infected straight woman
NF_S = noninfected straight woman

infected. Only when one partner is infected and the other is not is there any possibility of transmission. As Table 6.2 shows, there are eight pairings in which an infected partner has sex with a noninfected partner; these are the pairings in which it is possible for AIDS to be transmitted.

The exact risks involved in intercourse between infected and non-infected partners are unknown; therefore, modeling the sexual transmission of AIDS necessarily carries us beyond hard evidence and into a more speculative realm. There is some evidence that the transmission probability (T) of AIDS in a single act of intercourse between two men differs from the transmission probability for a single act of male-female intercourse. Further, within heterosexual intercourse, the probability of the virus being transmitted from an infected man to a noninfected woman is apparently greater than the probability of transmission from an infected woman to a noninfected man. Hence the model assumes three different transmission probabilities: TMM (the probability of transmission from an infected man to a noninfected man for any single act of intercourse); TMF (the probability of transmission from an infected man to a noninfected woman for any single act of intercourse); and TFM (the probability of transmission from an infected woman to a noninfected man for any single act of intercourse). Table 6.3, building on Table 6.2, lists the types of intercourse in which AIDS can be transmitted, along with the relevant transmission probabilities.

With regard to these transmission probabilities, apparently there is no difference between sex between two homosexual men, on the one hand, and between a homosexual man and a bisexual man, on the other. This is not to say, however, that the distinction between gay and bisexual men is irrelevant, because only bisexual men sexually transfer the virus into the heterosexual population. It also could be that because male bisexuals have sex with women as well as with men, their frequency of sex with men is lower than that of homosexual men, who do not have sex with women. Still, for any particular act of intercourse between two males, the gay male and bisexual male populations are indistinguishable. Hence, for the purpose of calculating the number of new sexually transmitted AIDS infections during a particular time period, we combine infected gays and bisexuals into a single group, denoted as IM_{GB}.

Table 6.3

Transmission Probabilities for Each Type of
Pairing for Which AIDS Can Be Transmitted

Intercourse Type	Relevant Transmission Probability
(1) $IM_G \times NM_G$	TMM
(2) $IM_G \times NM_B$	TMM
(3) $NM_G \times IM_B$	TMM
(4) $IM_B \times NM_B$	TMM
(5) $IM_B \times NF_S$	TMF
(6) $NM_B \times IF_S$	TFM
(7) $IM_S \times NF_S$	TMF
(8) $NM_S \times IF_S$	TFM

NOTE: IM_G = infected gay man
NM_G = noninfected gay man
IM_B = infected bisexual man
NM_B = noninfected bisexual man
IM_S = infected straight man
NM_S = noninfected straight man
IF_S = infected straight woman
NF_S = noninfected straight woman

Of course, the probability of contracting AIDS from any single act of intercourse is not the same as the probability of becoming infected during a particular time period. The probability (P) that a noninfected person will become infected during a particular time period from sex with an infected partner is a function not only of the transmission probability for a single act of intercourse, but also of the number of different relationships (R) in which the person engages during the time period and the frequency (F) of sexual intercourse within each relationship.

PM_G, PM_B, PM_S, and PF_S are the probabilities that a sexually active noninfected gay man, bisexual man, heterosexual man, and heterosexual woman, respectively, will become infected during any particular time period through sex with an infected partner. Since women can be infected by bisexuals and by heterosexuals, PF_S is the sum of PF_SMB (the probability of becoming infected by a bisexual male) and PF_SMS (the probability of becoming infected by a heterosexual man). Table 6.4 displays the terms needed to calculate the transmission probabilities for each group (i.e., the probabilities that a sexually active infected person will infect a noninfected member of a particular group during the time period in question). To convert the T, F, and R terms into the P term for each group, it is easiest to think of the probability of nontransmission

Table 6.4

Per Time Period Probabilities of a Sexually Active Noninfected Person in Relevant Groups Becoming Infected

Group	Period Probability (P)	Transmission Probability (T)	Average Frequency of Intercourse per Time Period (F)	Average Number of Relationships per Time Period (R)
Gays	$PM_G M_G$	$TM_G M_G$	$FM_G M_G$	$RM_G M_G$
Bisexuals from gays	$PM_B M_G$	$TM_G M_G$	$FM_B M_G$	$RM_B M_G$
Bisexuals from females	$PM_B F_S$	$TF_S M_S$	$FM_B F_S$	$RM_B F_S$
Heterosexual males from females	$PM_S F_S$	$TF_S M_S$	$FM_S F_S$	$RM_S F_S$
Females from bisexuals	$PF_S M_B$	$TM_B F_S$	$FM_B F_S$	$RM_B F_S$
Females from heterosexuals	$PF_S M_S$	$TM_S F_S$	$FM_S F_S$	$RM_S F_S$

NOTE: The T, F, and R terms are converted to the P term according to the following formula:
$$P = 1 - (1 - T)^{F \times R}$$

of the AIDS virus in a given act of intercourse. The T, F, and R terms then can be converted to P as follows:

$$P = 1 - (1 - T)^{F \times R}$$

Since the probability of transmission is T (say, .01), the probability of nontransmission must be $1 - T$ (.99). Thus, if one engaged in sex, say, four times with each of two partners (i.e., if F and $R = 4$ and 2, respectively), for a total of eight acts of intercourse, the probability of not transmitting AIDS in any of those eight acts would be $(1 - T)^{F \times R}$, or $(.99)^8$. Since the probability that AIDS would not be transmitted during the period is .923, the probability that it would be transmitted is $1 - .923$, or .077.

Table 6.5 examines the sensitivity of P, the probability that during a given period a sexually active infected person will transmit the AIDS virus to a previously noninfected person, to different hypothetical probabilities of AIDS transmission per act, frequency of intercourse during the period, and number of sex partners during the period. Assuming, for example, that the probability of transmitting AIDS in a single act is only .001, that the potential transmitter has only one noninfected

Table 6.5

Sensitivity of P (Per Time Period Probability for a Sexually Active Non-infected Person Becoming Infected from Sex with Infected Partner[s]) to T (Transmission Probability), F (Average Frequency of Intercourse per Relationship), and R (Average Number of Relationships)

T	R	F	P	T	R	F	P	T	R	F	P	T	R	F	P
.001	1	1	.001	.01	1	1	.01	.1	1	1	.10	.2	1	1	.20
.001	1	2	.002	.01	1	2	.02	.1	1	2	.19	.2	1	2	.36
.001	1	5	.005	.01	1	5	.05	.1	1	5	.41	.2	1	5	.67
.001	1	10	.010	.01	1	10	.10	.1	1	10	.65	.2	1	10	.89
.001	1	20	.020	.01	1	20	.20	.1	1	20	.88	.2	1	20	.99
.001	2	1	.002	.01	2	1	.02	.1	2	1	.19	.2	2	1	.36
.001	2	2	.004	.01	2	5	.10	.1	2	2	.34	.2	2	2	.59
.001	2	5	.010	.01	2	10	.18	.1	2	5	.65	.2	2	5	.89
.001	2	10	.020	.01	2	20	.33	.1	2	10	.88	.2	2	10	.99
.001	5	1	.005	.01	5	1	.05	.1	5	1	.41	.2	5	1	.67
.001	5	2	.010	.01	5	2	.10	.1	5	2	.65	.2	5	2	.89
.001	5	5	.025	.01	5	5	.22	.1	5	5	.93	.2	5	5	1.00
.001	10	1	.010	.01	10	1	.10	.1	10	1	.65	.2	10	1	.89
.001	10	2	.020	.01	10	2	.18	.1	10	2	.88	.2	10	2	.99
.001	20	1	.020	.01	20	1	.18	.1	20	1	.88	.2	20	1	.99
.001	20	2	.039	.01	20	2	.33	.1	20	2	.99	.2	20	2	1.00

sex partner during the relevant period, and that the potential transmitter and his or her partner engage in intercourse only once during the period, the probability of transmitting AIDS is only .001. If we hold the per-act transmission probability constant at .001 and increase the number of sex partners from 1 to 20 and the average frequency of intercourse per partner from 1 to 2, we see that the probability that the infected individual will transmit the disease during the period climbs dramatically, from .001 to .039. Even more dramatic increases, however, are registered when we adjust the per-act transmission probability. Indeed, at relatively high rates of transmission for a single act (represented in Table 6.5 by T values of .1 or .2), multiple relationships rapidly lead to a greater than 50% probability of infection during the time period, and in some circumstances to a near certainty of infection.

Table 6.6 develops prediction equations for new sexually transmitted AIDS cases per time period for each relevant population. These are the

Table 6.6
Equations for New Cases of AIDS Infection from
Sexual Activity per Month for Different Groups

Additional gay men:

$$IM_G^{(t+1)} = IM_{GB}^t \times (IM_G^t/IM_{GB}^t) \times PM_G M_G$$

Additional bisexual men, infected by gay men:

$$IM_{BG}^{(t+1)} = (IM_{GB}^t) \times (IM_B^t/IM_{GB}^t) \times PM_B M_G$$

Additional bisexual men, infected by heterosexual women:

$$IM_B F_S^{(t+1)} = (IF_S^t) \times PM_B F_S$$

Total additional bisexual men:

$$IM_B^{(t+1)} = IM_B M_G^{(t+1)} + IM_B F_S^{(t+1)}$$

Additional heterosexual men:

$$IM_S^{(t+1)} = IF_S^t \times PM_S F_S$$

Additional heterosexual women, infected by bisexual men:

$$IF_S M_B^{(t+1)} = IM_B^t \times PF_S M_B$$

Additional heterosexual women, infected by heterosexual men:

$$IF_S M_S^{(t+1)} = IF_S M_S^t \times PF_S M_S$$

Total additional heterosexual women:

$$IF_S^{(t+1)} = IF_S M_B^{(t+1)} + IF_S M_S^{(t+1)}$$

---

equations that actually drive the simulation model. To solve the equations, the initial infection incidence for each population (the "I" terms in Table 6.6) must first be supplied. These beginning values then can be multiplied by the population-specific infection probability for a given period (the "P" terms described in Table 6.4).

The simulation begins with 50,000 infected individuals—a fairly realistic starting point, given the mid-1987 estimate of 35,000 sexually transmitted AIDS cases in the United States. The next question relates to the initial composition of the population of infected persons. Of the 50,000 carriers of the disease, how many are homosexual men? How many are bisexual men? And how many are heterosexual men or women? If our purposes were to produce realistic parameter estimates of the group-specific incidence of AIDS in some future year, we would need to begin with reliable figures on the sizes of these four groups. We are not aware of the existence of such information, however.

We must therefore set the group-specific initial infection incidence figures simply by assumption. We begin by assuming that the AIDS virus is initially transmitted only by homosexual and bisexual males—that heterosexual men and women are not in the original pool of transmitters—and, more specifically, that of the original transmitters, most (31,250 of the 50,000) are homosexuals and the rest (18,750 of the 50,000) are bisexuals. Of course, other assumptions are possible, and we incorporate several other assumptions into the simulation model in the form of the alternative group-specific I terms shown in Table 6.7.

Now the task becomes moving from these initial infection figures to the end of the simulated time period which, for convenience, we set at one year or 12 one-month cycles. What remains is the specification of the P terms, and here we are brought back, finally, to the policy issues that gave rise to this exercise in the first place.

These policy issues are embodied in the simulation model in the terms that combine to form the group-specific P values. The extent to which the spread of AIDS could be slowed by policies that encourage sexually monogamous relationships can be gauged by noting how sensitive the transmission of the disease is to variations in the R term—the number of partners with whom an infected individual engages in sex per month. In the simulation, three alternative R values are specified, representing one, two, or three different sex partners per month. The extent to which the spread of AIDS could be slowed by policies that encourage sexual abstinence or restraint can be gauged by noting how sensitive disease transmission is to variations in the F term—the frequency of intercourse per partner per month. In the simulation, three alternative F values are specified, representing 4, 8, or 12 acts of intercourse per month. The extent to which the spread of AIDS could be slowed by encouraging AIDS testing, thereby alerting people that they are infected with the AIDS virus and lowering their sexual contact with noninfected people, can be gauged by noting how sensitive disease transmission is to variations in the R and F terms together. And the extent to which the spread of AIDS could be slowed by policies that encourage the use of condoms and other physical protection can be gauged by noting how sensitive disease transmission is to variations in the T terms—the probability of transmitting the disease in a given sexual encounter. In the simulation, two alternative sets of group-specific per-act transmission probabilities are specified, assuming (conservatively, we believe)

Table 6.7
Computer Simulation Independent Variables and Values

Variable		Values or Levels
T	Per-act transmission probability	1. Without condom $TGG = .01$ $TFM = .001$ $TMF = .005$ 2. With condom $TGG = .005$ $TFM = .0005$ $TMF = .0025$
F	Average frequency of intercourse per month per relationship	1. 4 times (once a week) 2. 8 times (twice a week) 3. 12 times (3 times a week)
R	Average number of relationships per month	1. 1 relationship 2. 2 relationships 3. 3 relationships
I	Initial infection incidence	1. $IG = 31250$ $IB = 18750$ $IM = 0$ $IF = 0$ 2. $IG = 12500$ $IB = 12500$ $IM = 12500$ $IF = 12500$ 3. $IG = 50000$ $IB = 0$ $IM = 0$ $IF = 0$

that transmission of AIDS is twice as likely in the absence of a condom or other physical protection as when such protection is employed.

RESULTS

We built a computer model based on the prediction equations in the form of the simple BASIC program listed in Table 6.8. As noted above,

Table 6.8
Listing of the BASIC Model

```
10  REM A simulation of the sexual transmission
20  REM of AIDS
30  REM Set transmission probabilities per act per group
40  COUNT = 1
50  FOR T = 1 TO 2
60    IF T = 2 THEN GOTO 120
70    REM Transmission probability per act without condoms
80      TGG = .01                    'gay to gay'
90      TFM = .001                   'female to male'
100     TMF = .005                   'male to female'
110     GOTO 160
120    REM Transmission probability per act with condoms
130     TGG = .005
140     TFM = .0005
150     TMF = .0025
160  REM Set Frequencies of intercourse per month per relationship
170  FOR F = 1 TO 3
180    IF F = 2 THEN GOTO 230
190    IF F = 3 THEN GOTO 260
200  REM freq = 4 = once a week
210    FG = 4 : FBG = 4 : FBF = 4 : FMF = 4
220    GOTO 290
230  REM freq = 8 = twice a week
240    FG = 8 : FBG = 8 : FBF = 8 : FMF = 8
250    GOTO 290
260  REM freq =12 = three times a week
270    FG = 12 : FBG = 12 : FBF = 12 : FMF = 12
280    GOTO 290
290  REM Set number of relationships per group
300  FOR R = 1 TO 3
310    IF R = 2 THEN GOTO 350
320    IF R = 3 THEN GOTO 370
330  RG = 1 :  RBG = 1 : RBF = 1 :  RMF = 1
340    GOTO 380
350  RG = 2 :  RBG = 2 : RBF = 2 :  RMF = 2
360    GOTO 380
370  RG = 3 :  RBG = 3 : RBF = 3 :  RMF = 3
380    REM # infected in different groups
390  FOR I = 1 TO 3
400    IF I = 2 THEN GOTO 440
410    IF I = 3 THEN 460
420  IB = 18750  :  IG = 31250  :  IW =    0  :  IM =    0
430    GOTO 480
440  IB = 12500  :  IG = 12500  :  IW = 12500  :  IM = 12500
450    GOTO 480
460  IB =    0  :  IG = 50000  :  IW =    0  :  IM =    0
470    GOTO 480
480    REM Calculating incidence for a year
490    FOR MONTH = 1 TO 12    'per month trans. prob. per group'
500      PGG = 1-(1-TGG)^(FG*RG)      'gays from gays'
```

(continued)

Table 6.8 (Continued)

```
510      PBG = 1-(1-TGG)^(FBG*RBG)        'bisexuals from gays'
520      PBF = 1-(1-TFM)^(FBF*RBG)        'bisexuals from females'
530      PMF = 1-(1-TFM)^(FMF*RMF)        'heterosexual males from females'
540      PFB = 1-(1-TMF)^(FBF*RBF)        'females from bisexuals'
550      PFM = 1-(1-TMF)^(FMF*RMF)        'females from heterosexuals'
560   IG = IG + (IG * PGG) + (IB * PBG)
570   IB = IB + (IG * PBG) + (IW * PFB)
580   IM = IM + (IW * PMF)
590   IW = IW + (IM * PFM) + (IB * PFB)
600   IG = INT(IG) :  IB = INT(IB)  :  IM = INT(IM) :  IW = INT(IW)
610     NEXT MONTH
620    PRINT COUNT; T; F; R; I; IG; IB; IM; IW
630    LPRINT COUNT; T; F; R; I; IG; IB; IM; IW
640   COUNT = COUNT + 1
650     NEXT I
660     NEXT R
670     NEXT F
680     NEXT T
690   END
```

four independent variables were tested: T, the probability of infection per single act of intercourse; F, the average frequency of intercourse per relationship per month; R, the average number of relationships per month; and I, the group-specific initial infection incidence. Since one of these independent variables contains two levels while the other three contain three levels each, the total number of cases when all possible combinations of independent variables are tested is $2 \times 3 \times 3 \times 3 = 54$.

The simulation results are presented in Table 6.9 in the form of the average number of new AIDS cases at the end of 12 months for each level of each independent variable. In the table, each variable is fixed at a particular level while the other variables vary. This presentation ignores the interactive effects of the independent variables. Multivariate analyses not reported here indicate, however, that the lion's share of the impacts are in the form of main effects rather than interactions, and that the interactive effects do not detract from the impacts shown in the table. In this light, we have opted for the simple mode of presentation employed in Table 6.9.

For any given sexual encounter, the model assumes that the use of a condom or other protective device halves the probability of transmitting AIDS; however, in the first two rows of Table 6.9 we see that over the course of 12 months the use of such devices does much more than halve the incidence of AIDS. When the higher per-act transmission probabilities associated with not using condoms or other physical protection are assumed, the total number of new AIDS infections after a year works out to almost 2.5 million—a 50-fold increase over the original 50,000 cases. When the lower per-act transmission probabilities associated with use of condoms or other physical protection are assumed, the number of new infections drops to "only" about 325,000—still a substantial increase from the original 50,000 cases, but an order of magnitude beneath the consequences of failing to take physical precautions.

How could merely halving the per-act transmission probability yield, at the end of a year, such an enormous difference in the number of new AIDS cases? The answer is that a compounding process is at work. If, say, twice as many people are infected during the first month of the year, then twice as many people are capable of transmitting the disease during the second month, and so on through the end of the year.

In setting the group-specific T values, we deliberately made a conservative assumption about the effect of condoms or other physical protection on the per-act AIDS transmission probability; that is, we assumed that T was only twice as great without protection as with it. A key insight to be derived from the simulation results, then, is that even on the basis of this conservative assumption it appears that policies designed to encourage the use of condoms or other protective devices can play a key role in slowing the spread of AIDS. If anything, the results summarized in Table 6.9 probably understate the potential impact of such policies.

What about the impact of the remaining terms in the model? The frequency of intercourse involving an infected person (F) and the number of relationships involving an infected person (R) have the same impact on the monthly transmission probability. When either the frequency of intercourse within a relationship or the number of different relationships is high (12 times per month, or three different partners per month), the total infection incidence soars to 3,215,288. At the other extreme, when either the frequency of intercourse within a relationship or the number of relationships is low (once a week, or one relationship per month), the number of new infections drops to 189,036. Obviously, then, frequent and widespread intercourse between those infected with the AIDS virus and those not previously infected greatly accelerates the spread of AIDS.

Table 6.9
Incidence of Infection After One Year

Variable	Level	IM_G	IM_B	IM_S	IF_S	Total
T	1	1,080,835	958,156	27,660	412,524	2,479,176
	2	163,660	116,401	6,076	40,466	326,603
F	1	99,439	63,802	5,011	20,784	189,036
	2	378,965	300,750	10,215	114,413	804,343
	3	1,388,339	1,247,282	35,379	544,288	3,215,288
R	1	99,439	63,802	5,011	20,784	189,036
	2	378,965	300,750	10,215	114,413	804,343
	3	1,388,339	1,247,282	35,379	544,288	3,215,288
I	1	694,327	602,074	13,416	246,814	1,556,631
	2	373,850	338,069	22,925	162,199	897,044
	3	798,566	671,693	14,263	270,472	1,754,993

Lowest incidence ($T = 2, F = 1, R = 1, I = 2$)

		19,741	18,019	12,830	15,841	66,431

Highest incidence ($T = 1, F = 3, R = 3, I = 3$)

		7,481,643	6,987,352	178,058	3,146,520	17,793,573

As noted above, we know of no reliable figures on the composition of the AIDS-infected population, in terms of how many are homosexual men, how many are bisexual men, and how many are heterosexual men or women. That being the case, we set the group-specific initial infection incidence by making assumptions that have no firm empirical foundation. Happily for the simulation, however, Table 6.9 indicates that number of new AIDS infections varies relatively little as a function of the value of I, the term representing the composition of those initially infected. Comparing the variability in AIDS infections associated with different I values to the variability associated with different T, F, and R values suggests that I is, by a considerable distance, the least important of the four independent variables—an impression borne out in multivariate analyses not reported here. This is a pleasing result methodologically, since it means that setting what amount to arbitrary values for this variable has had a relatively minimal impact on the simulation results. More substantively, this means that the crucial variable in the spread of AIDS is not the initial incidence pattern for the disease.

According to our results, the year-end incidence of AIDS is highest when those initially infected are either all gay men or are a mix of gay and bisexual men, but these composition-based differences are not decisive.

From a policy perspective, the crucial question concerns the relative leverage the T, F, and R variables provide over the spread of the disease. What does the model suggest about the point or points at which policies intended to restrict the spread of AIDS might do the most good? Of course, we must bear in mind that although we consider the values assigned to these variables in the simulation reasonable, they are rather arbitrary; thus, for example, assuming that a potential AIDS carrier engages in sex with three different people per month may be unrealistically liberal, while assuming that the use of condoms or other physical protection only halves the transmission rate may be unrealistically conservative. Still, for the values that we employed in the simulation, the per-act transmission rate displays a somewhat less extreme effect on the spread of the disease than does either the average frequency of intercourse per relationship or the average number of relationships. The policy implication is that campaigns designed to encourage sexual restraint and AIDS testing, which if successful would lead to drops in sexual activity among those at risk, are apt to have a somewhat greater payoff than campaigns for "safe sex." Of course, this conclusion is provisional, subject to reconsideration should firmer data become available upon which to build the model's assumptions.

More generally, the simulation results strongly suggest that policies such as encouraging AIDS testing, sexual abstinence or restraint, and sexual monogamy could all have a pronounced effect on the incidence of AIDS. It should be noted, however, that even if these policies were successful, the spread of AIDS would by no means be arrested. Indeed, even if we make the most favorable set of assumptions available in the model (that the per-act transmission probabilities are those associated with use of condoms or other physical protection; that the average monthly frequency of intercourse per relationship and the average monthly number of relationships are both minimal; and that the initial infection incidence is equally spread among the four population groups), we see in Table 6.9 that by the end of the year there would be 66,431 new AIDS cases, more than doubling the number at the start of the year. On the other hand, this "best case" scenario is much more favorable than its "worst case" counterpart: as opposed to the 66,431 new AIDS cases associated with the most favorable conditions, the least favorable combination of conditions (high per-act transmission rates high frequency and number of relationships; and initial restriction of the virus to homosexual men alone) would result in a total of 17,793,573 new cases by the end of the year.

CONCLUSION

The primary difficulty in constructing a model of the sexual transmission of AIDS lies not in developing prediction equations, which is a relatively straightforward exercise, but in establishing plausible values for the input variables. Only very sketchy empirical evidence is available to guide our specifications for the per-act transmission probabilities (T); the number of sexual relationships between infected and noninfected individuals (R); the frequency of intercourse within a relationship (F); and the initial incidence of infection for each group (I). If the values assumed in our simulation are grossly unrealistic, then our simulation results would not be especially useful for policy purposes. Even in that case, however, the model could be heuristically useful, directing attention toward potentially fruitful policies and toward pressing data needs. And for present purposes the model provides a straightforward application of computer simulation modeling to the analysis of a complex social problem.

7

Simulation #3—An Exercise Incorporating Stochastic Variation

In the final illustrative simulation exercise (drawn from Sigelman and Whicker, 1987), we formulate a model of the peer review process that is used in evaluating manuscripts submitted for publication in scholarly journals. The simulation focuses on the implications of various types of potential bias in peer review, including conventionality on the part of reviewers, and tendencies for editors to extend preferential treatment to work that is similar to their own research and to accord preferential treatment to prestigious authors. Whereas the simulations in Chapters 5 and 6 have been deterministic, this one is stochastic.

THE PROBLEM

An important component of the process by which scholarly research is published is peer review, the assessment of the research by a set of experts. The basic purpose of peer review is to weed out research that is not meritorious by subjecting work that is submitted to quality testing. There is, however, a widespread perception that manuscript reviews by "peers" of the manuscript's author tend to confer an unfair advantage on established scholars who work within a field's accepted paradigm, at the expense of less established scholars pursuing less conventional research agendas—all to the detriment of the quality and diversity of work published in a scholarly field.

We wondered about the widely held perception that factors other than a manuscript's intrinsic merit help determine whether it is published. Suppose, as is widely believed, that biases do crop up in the evaluation of manuscripts. What impact would these biases have? To what extent would they affect the quality and diversity of published work?

In order to probe these issues, we decided to undertake a computer simulation of bias in peer review. Why study these issues via computer simulation rather than a more standard empirically based analysis? Largely because empirical data are inapplicable to the issues at hand.

Not only are data bearing on these issues presently unavailable; it is impossible *in principle* that they will become available. The first requisite of an empirical analysis of the impact of bias on the merit of published work is a measure of merit that exists apart from scholars' evaluations (i.e., that is independent of peer review). The very rationale for peer review, however, is that merit cannot be established in any absolute sense; because there is no objective standard, the scholarly community opts for intersubjective evaluation. In the absence of an objective measure of worth, which is unavailable in the absence of a review written by God, an empirical assessment of the impact of peer review on the quality of published work would be subject to the very biases it purports to study. Accordingly, we decided to proceed by laying out various possibilities and then exploring their logical implications. For this task, computer simulation is ideally suited.

THE MODEL

Verbal Formulation

We began with a simple story—an overview, in effect, of the peer review process. That process begins when a manuscript arrives at the office of the editor of a journal. The editor initially examines the manuscript closely enough to determine that it is reviewable and to select reviewers, to whom she sends the manuscript along with instructions and forms. After the reviewers respond, she decides whether to accept or reject the manuscript for publication, based on the reviewers' assessments and her own view of it. This same sequence recurs many times during a given year. In social science, it usually culminates in an editorial decision to reject the manuscript. Rejection rates of 80% or more are commonplace in social science, and the most highly regarded journals reject more than 90% of the papers they receive.

Our story posed a somewhat simplified or stylized version of the peer review process. Simplification is, as we noted earlier, an inherent part of modeling, and the main challenge is to avoid losing essential features of the underlying process in the process of simplification. Our primary simplifications focused on the motivations of the editor and the reviewers.

According to our telling, the editor's chief task is to try to assure that the journal prints the best manuscripts it receives. In performing this task the editor relies heavily on the reviewers' assessments. Indeed, we assume that the editor does not make an independent judgment of the quality of a manuscript. Rather, she selects as reviewers experts whose opinions she respects and then defers to their collective expertise. However, the editor also can supplement the reviewers' evaluations with other available information. We highlight two such items—the editor's view of a manuscript's "suitability" for the journal and her deference toward the manuscript's author.

The editor may be open to publishing papers that span a diversity of intellectual traditions, substantive foci, and methodological orientations. Such a catholic editor would be willing to publish any manuscript, space permitting, if the review process suggests that it is sufficiently meritorious. On the other hand, the editor may have a narrower conception of what is most suitable for her journal. A parochial editor views a manuscript from the perspective of her own intellectual, substantive, and methodological orientations. If a favorably reviewed manuscript is too far removed from the editor's own interests, she discounts the reviewers' assessments of the manuscript's quality and may end up rejecting it.

The manuscript's "bloodlines" also may influence the editor. A submission from a highly regarded scholar may enjoy a competitive advantage because the editor uses the author's prior accomplishments as an indicator of the manuscript's quality, or because the editor wants to enhance the journal's visibility and reputation by publishing articles by leading scholars, or even because the editor hopes to ingratiate herself with influential members of the profession. For a given editor such considerations may place no role at all, but for another editor they may rank alongside the reviewers' evaluations in determining whether a manuscript is publishable.

We assume that the author's identity is unknown to, and cannot be inferred by, the reviewers; that is, we assume that a "blind review" process is in place, as is true of most scholarly journals. Reviewers, however, still can be affected by factors other than a manuscript's intrinsic quality. For example, some reviewers tend to be harsher and others more lenient. More important, different reviewers have different scholarly outlooks. Some welcome challenges to or departures from approaches, methods, and ideas that currently hold sway, while others, more wedded to the status quo, react negatively to what they perceive as attacks on conventional outlooks and approaches. Both the reviewers' harshness or leniency and their orientation toward the dominant paradigm can influence their evaluations of a manuscript's merit.

Formalization

Next, we formalized this verbal overview of the peer review process. Formalization in the simulation context parallels operationalization in the context of standard empirical data analysis, in that both move from the realm of the abstract into the realm of the concrete.

We decided, for purposes of the simulation, that we would focus on a quarterly journal to which 60 manuscripts are submitted during a 3-month period. We could just as well have decided upon a monthly journal that receives more articles, but settled upon quarterly and 60 because these appeared to be reasonably typical of social science journals. From these 60 manuscripts our hypothetical editor must select 10 to appear in an upcoming issue. We settled on 10 because that seemed a reasonable number for an issue and because the acceptance rate of one in six would make this journal reasonably representative of social science journals. Each of the 60 hypothetical manuscripts would have four relevant characteristics: its *conventionality,* its *quality, the prestige of its author,* and its *interest to the editor.* In the simulation, each of these characteristics would be represented by a variable that ranges from a low score of 1 to a high of 6. Of course, there is nothing magic about a 1-6 scale; we could just as well have chosen 1-10, 1-100, or any number of other scales. We decided further that each manuscript's score on each dimension would be randomly drawn from a "quasi-normal" distribution of 12 possible scores between 1 and 6 (1, 2, 2, 3, 3, 3, 4, 4, 4, 5, 5, 6). This assumption of quasi-normality is consistent with the observation of many journal editors that most submissions fall into a gray middle area, with relatively few that are truly outstanding and relatively few that are truly dreadful.

Referring back to our verbal formulation of the process, we decided that the editor would send every manuscript to three reviewers, each of whom has two relevant characteristics. *Severity* would be scored on a scale ranging from 1 (for a reviewer who is very lenient) to 6 (for one who is very harsh). In the simulation, severity scores actually are trichotomized so that a given reviewer is classified as either lenient (for those with a severity score of 1 or 2); harsh (a score of 5 or 6); or neither (a score of 3 or 4). What difference does severity make? We decided to assume that a lenient reviewer would assign a quality rating 1.5 points above a manuscript's true quality (as defined in the preceding paragraph), up to a maximum rating of 6; a harsh reviewer would assign a quality rating 1.5 points below the manuscript's true quality, down to a minimum of 1; and a reviewer who is neither lenient nor harsh would assign the manuscript's true quality rating.

The second reviewer characteristic is *conventionality*, or the strength of a reviewer's tie to the dominant paradigm in her subfield, also measured on a 1-6 scale. If the reviewer is more conventional than the manuscript is, her rating of the manuscript is adversely affected. Operationally, a manuscript conventionality score lower than the reviewer's conventionality score becomes a ceiling on the reviewer's rating of the manuscript. The idea is that because a reviewer's assessment of the quality of a manuscript is affected by her assessment of the manuscript's suitability, from the reviewer's perspective the manuscript can be no better than it is suitable. On the other hand, if the reviewer's conventionality score is less than or equal to that of the manuscript, she averages the manuscript's conventionality score and her own assessment of the manuscript's quality to produce a rating of the manuscript.

Reviewer severity scores are drawn randomly from the same "quasi-normal" distribution described above; accordingly, most reviewers are neither lenient nor harsh. Random selection from the same distribution is also used to set a reviewer's conventionality score. Because we were especially interested in the impact of reviewer conventionality on the quality and diversity of published articles, however, we decided to experiment with two other distributions of reviewer conventionality scores: a distribution skewed toward unconventional reviewers (with conventionality scores of 1, 1, 1, 1, 2, 2, 2, 3, 3, 4, 5, 6) and one skewed toward conventional reviewers (1, 2, 3, 4, 4, 5, 5, 5, 6, 6, 6, 6). Our use of these three different distributions parallels an experimental treatment or manipulation in a standard experimental design.

As we noted in earlier chapters, often it can be quite useful for the modeler to prepare a flowchart of the underlying process. We demonstrated such a flowchart in Chapter 5. For present purposes, a contingency table serves much the same purpose of schematizing the process; hence in Table 7.1 we summarize the peer review process from the perspective of a reviewer. Given a certain "true quality" score for a given manuscript, the advice a reviewer of the manuscript passes along to the editor varies as a function of the reviewer's severity (low, medium, or high) and the reviewer's conventionality relative to that of the manuscript (higher than that of the manuscript or lower than that of the manuscript). The contingency table simply displays all the "if-then" combinations that are possible. The simulation works from the algorithms specified in the margins of the contingency table and supplies the values in the cells. To see how this works, suppose that a manuscript with a true quality rating of 4 is sent to a reviewer with a high severity rating. That severe reviewer begins by assigning a quality rating of 2.5 to the manuscript, 1.5 below its "true" score. Suppose further that the manuscript is extremely unconventional, with a score of only 2 on the 1-6 conventionality scale, and that the reviewer is much more conventional. In that case, the reviewer downgrades the manuscript even farther, assigning it a final score of only 2.0 and returning that rating to the editor.

The editor also has two relevant characteristics, *openness* and *deference*. Her judgment of a manuscript's quality is unaffected by her conventionality or severity, because we assumed above that she makes no independent judgment concerning quality. She can, however, supplement or discount the reviewers' evaluations with other judgments of her own. Thus an editor whose scholarly vision is restricted to her own subfield and its nearest neighbors may view more distant work as less deserving of publication; the more a manuscript departs from her own interests, the less inclined she is to publish it. On the other hand, a more eclectic editor may exhibit no perceptible territoriality, welcoming well-reviewed manuscripts irrespective of subfield.

The editor's openness, treated as a dichotomy, constitutes the second experimental manipulation in the model. An editor who does not judge manuscripts in terms of her own interests makes publication decisions on the basis of the reviewers' assessments, perhaps (as we shall see momentarily) factoring in the author's prestige as well. The model determines whether the editor employs the personal interest criterion by first assuming that she does not and generating a full set of editorial decisions, and then assuming that she does and generating new decisions on the same manuscripts. In the latter case, the editor who is more warmly disposed to manuscripts that are of more immediate personal interest uses the manuscript's personal interest score to supplement the reviewers' assessments, giving this interest score a weight equal to a single review—sufficient weight to nudge a manuscript either higher or lower in the acceptance queue.

The editor's sensitivity to authorial prestige is treated in the model in a manner similar to her openness. That is, we first assume that the author's prestige makes no difference to the editor, who pays it no heed when deciding whether to publish the manuscript; that decision is determined by the reviewers' ratings, supplemented for certain editors by the manuscript's interest to the editor. We then assume that the editor *is* influenced by the author's prestige. In that case, the editor uses the author's prestige score to supplement the reviewer's ratings; of course,

Table 7.1
Reviewer's Decision-Making Contingencies

Reviewer's Severity	Reviewer's Relative Conventionality		
	Reviewer conventionality less than or equal to manuscript	Reviewer conventionality greater than manuscript	
Low			Quality = true quality + 1.5
Medium			Quality = true quality
High			Quality = true quality − 1.5
	Quality = conventionality + severity-weighted quality index	Maximum quality = manuscript conventionality	

the editor who cares about the degree of interest she has in the manuscript *and* the author's prestige uses both to supplement the reviewers' ratings.

Thus the simulation focuses on editors who use four different decision rules: one is influenced by neither interest nor prestige, and gives equal weight to each reviewer's rating of the manuscript; the second is influenced by interest but not prestige, and gives equal weight to each reviewer's rating and the manuscript's interest score; the third is influenced by prestige but not interest, and gives equal weight to each reviewer's rating and the author's prestige score; and the fourth is influenced by both interest and prestige, and gives equal weight to each reviewer's rating, the manuscript's interest score, and the author's prestige score. These combinations are laid out in contingency table form in Table 7.2. Having derived an overall rating of the manuscript, each type of editor selects for publication the 10 manuscripts with the highest overall scores from the 60 submitted during the quarter.

Now, what bearing might these factors have on the manuscripts published in our hypothetical journal? Our measure of the quality of the published work is the *mean true quality score* for manuscripts accepted for a quarterly issue. As measures of diversity, we focus on the *standard*

Table 7.2
Editor's Decision-Making Contingencies

| Editor's Deference | Editor's Interests | |
	Broad	Narrow
Low	Equal weight to each reviewer's rating	Equal weight to each reviewer's rating and to editor's interest in the manuscript
High	Equal weight to each reviewer's rating and to the author's prestige	Equal weight to each reviewer's rating, to the editor's interest in the manuscript, and to the author's prestige

deviation of the quality scores for accepted manuscripts, the *standard deviation of the author's prestige scores,* and the *standard deviation of the manuscript conventionality scores.* Although the means for accepted manuscripts on manuscript conventionality and author's prestige are not measures of diversity per se, we also shall discuss them in passing.

In the simulation, each type of editor operates in three different contexts, defined by the three different distributions of reviewer conventionality. Accordingly, in describing the outcomes of the review process, we employ a 3 (distribution of reviewer conventionality) × 2 (editor's weighting of personal interest) × 2 (editor's weighting of author's prestige) factorial design.

As indicated earlier, the values of the input variables are assigned by drawing in a random order from a given distribution of scores. Clearly, then, the simulation results are affected by the order in which values are drawn; for example, if three highly conventional reviewers are drawn consecutively for an unconventional manuscript, the manuscript's chances obviously are lower than if the same three reviewers are spaced out over three unconventional manuscripts. To counter any such order effects, we ran the model 10 times for each cell in the experimental design, bringing the total number of "cases" to 120—12 cells (3 × 2 × 2 = 12), with 10 sets of observations per cell. The case is defined as a quarter, during which 60 manuscripts are submitted to the journal; so while the number of cases on which the analysis focuses is 120, the manuscripts cycling through the simulated review system during these 120 quarters total 7,200. Because a given combination of input conditions was capable of yielding different outcomes depending on the order in which values were drawn (10 different outcomes, in fact), this is obviously a stochastic rather than deterministic model.

As with the simulations described in the last two chapters, we wrote a BASIC program representing this model (see Table 7.3 for a program listing). The program generated voluminous output, as we were dealing with 7,200 cases. We then performed statistical analyses on the data we had generated, using SPSSPC+. We prefer BASIC and SPSS because of their ready availability and ease of use, but the same results could have been achieved with a wide array of different software.

RESULTS

The characteristics of accepted and rejected manuscripts are compared in Table 7.4 across all 120 rounds. As would be expected, the accepted manuscripts are, on average, of higher quality than those that are declined. The mean quality score of the 10 accepted manuscripts in an average round is half a point higher on the 1-6 quality scale than the mean quality score of the 50 rejected manuscripts, and two out of every three accepted manuscripts have a true quality score of 4 or higher—well above the 47% for rejected manuscripts. To be sure, many low-quality manuscripts are accepted and many high-quality manuscripts are not. Still, these results are fairly reassuring, because they belie the image of the review process as a random crapshoot. Overall, the 120 quarterly review periods simulated here are reasonably successful in assuring that stronger manuscripts are published and weaker ones are not.

Across the 120 rounds, the mean manuscript conventionality and author's prestige scores also are higher for accepted than rejected manuscripts. In light of biases built into some of the experimental conditions—especially the editor's bias toward prestige—these results are hardly unexpected. On the other hand, the distribution skewed toward high reviewer conventionality is counterbalanced by another distribution equally skewed toward reviewer unconventionality. So why are accepted manuscripts so much more conventional than rejected manuscripts? This result stems from the decision rule reviewers employ vis-à-vis conventionality, which in effect leads a conventional reviewer to penalize an unconventional manuscript more than an unconventional reviewer penalizes a conventional manuscript. It is the deliberate asymmetry of the reviewer algorithm rather than the distribution of

Table 7.3
Listing of the BASIC Model

```
10 REM Peer Review Of Scientific
20 REM Activity Model
30 OPEN "o",#1,"data"
40 DIM D(3,12), A(4,12), AD(60), R(3), NPUB(11), PUB(11)
50 REM D is a data array of reviewer proclivities where
60 REM    i=1 is low skew; i=2 normal skew; i=3 high skew
70   D(1,1) = 1  :  D(2,1) = 1  :  D(3,1) = 1
80   D(1,2) = 1  :  D(2,2) = 2  :  D(3,2) = 2
90   D(1,3) = 1  :  D(2,3) = 2  :  D(3,3) = 3
100  D(1,4) = 1  :  D(2,4) = 3  :  D(3,4) = 4
110  D(1,5) = 2  :  D(2,5) = 3  :  D(3,5) = 4
120  D(1,6) = 2  :  D(2,6) = 3  :  D(3,6) = 5
130  D(1,7) = 2  :  D(2,7) = 4  :  D(3,7) = 5
140  D(1,8) = 3  :  D(2,8) = 4  :  D(3,8) = 5
150  D(1,9) = 3  :  D(2,9) = 4  :  D(3,9) = 6
160  D(1,10) = 4 :  D(2,10) = 5 :  D(3,10) = 6
170  D(1,11) = 5 :  D(2,11) = 5 :  D(3,11) = 6
180  D(1,12) = 6 :  D(2,12) = 6 :  D(3,12) = 6 :TN = 0
190 REM Independent Variables:
200 REM   RS: distribution of reviewer criticalness toward
210 REM        article paradigm suitability or conventionality
220 REM        low (1), normal  (2), or high (3) skew
230 REM   RQ: reviewer criticalness  of quality (1) skewed toward harsh;
240 REM        (2) normal  (3) skewed toward lenient
250 REM   EF: Focus of editor:  1=anything goes; 2=distance between
260 REM        editor interest and article area is averaged with reviewer
270 REM        scores; 3=editor focus score becomes a cap for article
280 REM   EP:  Weight placed by editor on prestige: 1 = no weight;
290 REM        2=prestige score averaged with reviewer scores
300 REM   No. of runs = 3 x 3 x 3 x 2 = 54
310 REM A is an array of article characteristics, where i=1 is
320 REM    focus; i=2 suitability; i=3 quality; i=4 author prestige
330  A(1,1) = 4  :  A(2,1) = 1  :  A(3,1) = 6 : A(4,1) = 1
340  A(1,2) = 4  :  A(2,2) = 6  :  A(3,2) = 5 : A(4,2) = 2
350  A(1,3) = 4  :  A(2,3) = 2  :  A(3,3) = 5 : A(4,3) = 2
360  A(1,4) = 5  :  A(2,4) = 2  :  A(3,4) = 4 : A(4,4) = 3
370  A(1,5) = 5  :  A(2,5) = 5  :  A(3,5) = 4 : A(4,5) = 3
380  A(1,6) = 6  :  A(2,6) = 5  :  A(3,6) = 4 : A(4,6) = 3
390  A(1,7) = 1  :  A(2,7) = 3  :  A(3,7) = 3 : A(4,7) = 4
400  A(1,8) = 2  :  A(2,8) = 4  :  A(3,8) = 3 : A(4,8) = 4
410  A(1,9) = 2  :  A(2,9) = 3  :  A(3,9) = 3 : A(4,9) = 4
420  A(1,10) = 3 :  A(2,10) = 4 :  A(3,10) = 2 : A(4,10) = 5
430  A(1,11) = 3 :  A(2,11) = 3 :  A(3,11) = 2 : A(4,11) = 5
440  A(1,12) = 3 :  A(2,12) = 4 :  A(3,12) = 1 : A(4,12) = 6
450 FOR RS = 1 TO 3      'loop for reviewer suitability decisions'
460 FOR RQ = 1 TO 3      'loop for reviewer quality decisions'
470 FOR EF = 1 TO 3      'loop for editor interest/focus'
480 FOR EP = 1 TO 2      'loop for editor weight on author prestige'
490  FOR I = 1 TO 60
500    AD(I) = 0     'AD = array of publishable scores and decisions'
```

(continued)

Table 7.3 (Continued)

```
510     NEXT I
520     N = 0    : P = 0     'n = counter; p = count of articles to be published'
530     FOR I = 1 TO 5
540     FOR J = 1 TO 12
550       X = ((I-1) * 12) + J                  '# of article, 1 <= x <= 60'
560      FOR M = 1 TO 3                  'reviewer decision on article x'
570       N = N + 1
580       IF N > 12 THEN N = 1
590       IF A(2,J) < D(RS,N) THEN 640
600       IF D(RQ,N) < 3 THEN R(M) = (A(2,J) + (A(3,J) - 1.5))/2   'RS<AS'
610       IF D(RQ,N) > 4 THEN R(M) = (A(2,J) + (A(3,J) + 1.5))/2
620       IF D(RQ,N) < 5 AND D(RQ,N) > 2 THEN R(M) = (A(2,J) + (A(3,J))/2
630       GOTO 650
640       R(M) = A(2,J)                          'AS > RS'
650       AD(X) = AD(X) + R(M)
660      NEXT M
670      AD(X) = AD(X)/3     'calc. average AS and AQ score for 3 reviewrs'
680     IF EF = 1 AND EP = 1 THEN 850      'editor decisions on article x'
690     IF EF = 1 AND EP = 2 THEN 740
700     IF EF = 2 AND EP = 1 THEN 760
710     IF EF = 2 AND EP = 2 THEN 780
720     IF EF = 3 AND EP = 1 THEN 800
730     IF EF = 3 AND EP = 2 THEN 830
740      AD(X) = (AD(X) * .75) + (A(4,J) * .25)  'no interest, prestige'
750       GOTO 850
760      AD(X) = (AD(X) *.75) +(6-(A(1,J)-D(2,J))*.25) 'distance int, no pr.'
770       GOTO 850
780     AD(X)=(AD(X)*.6)+((6-(A(1,J)-D(2,J)))*.2)+(A(4,J)*.2) 'distance int,
pr.'
790       GOTO 850
800      IF D(2,J) > A(1,J) THEN AD(X) = A(1,J)  'interest cap, no prestige'
810       ELSE AD(X) = (AD(X)*.75) + (A(1,J)*.25)
820       GOTO 850
830      IF D(2,J) > A(1,J) THEN AD(X) = A(1,J)  'interest cap, prestige'
840       ELSE AD(X) = (AD(X)*.6) + (A(1,J)*.2) + (A(4,J)*.2)
850     NEXT J
860     NEXT I
865    FOR X = 1 TO 60:   PRINT "ad(";X;") =";AD(X) : NEXT X
866    FOR X = 1 TO 60: LPRINT "ad(";X;") =";AD(X) : NEXT X
870     FOR X = 1 TO 60        'deciding which articles to publish'
880     IF AD(X) < 6 THEN 910
890     AD(X) = 99  : P = P + 1
900     IF P = 10 THEN 1160
910     NEXT X
911     FOR X = 1 TO 60        'deciding which articles to publish'
912     IF AD(X) < 5 OR AD(X) > = 6 THEN 915
913     AD(X) = 99  : P = P + 1
914     IF P = 10 THEN 1160
915     NEXT X
920     FOR X = 1 TO 60
930     IF AD(X) < 4 OR AD(X) > = 5   THEN 955
940     AD(X) = 99  : P = P + 1
950     IF P = 10 THEN 1160
```

(continued)

Table 7.3 (Continued)

```
955     NEXT X
960     FOR X = 1 TO 60
970     IF AD(X) < 3 OR AD(X) > = 4  THEN 1000
980     AD(X) = 99  : P = P + 1
990     IF P = 10 THEN 1160
1000    NEXT X
1010    FOR X = 1 TO 60
1020    IF AD(X) < 2 OR AD(X) > = 3  THEN 1050
1030    AD(X) = 99  : P = P + 1
1040    IF P = 10 THEN 1160
1050    NEXT X
1060    FOR X = 1 TO 60
1070    IF AD(X) < 1 OR AD(X) > = 2  THEN 1100
1080    AD(X) = 99  : P = P + 1
1090    IF P = 10 THEN 1160
1100    NEXT X
1110    FOR X = 1 TO 60
1120    IF AD(X) > = 1  THEN 1150
1130    AD(X) = 99  : P = P + 1
1140    IF P = 10 THEN 1160
1150    NEXT X
1155 PRINT              "p = ";P
1156 FOR X = 1 TO 60 :PRINT "        adr(";X;") =";AD(X) :NEXT X
1157 FOR X = 1 TO 60 :LPRINT "        adr(";X;") =";AD(X) :NEXT X
1160 REM Calculating dependent variables
1170 REM PUB = published article data; NPUB = not published article data
1180 REM  1-4=means for focus (1), suitability (2), quality 3), prestige (4)
1190 REM  5-8=std.dev. for same, same order
1200 REM  9 = proportion of articles with 6 quality score
1210 REM 10 = proportion of articles with 5 quality score
1220 REM 11 = proportion of articles with 4 quality score
1221 PRINT              "p = ";P
1222 LPRINT             "p = ";P
1223 FOR X = 1 TO 60 : PRINT "       adr(";X;") = ";AD(X) :NEXT X
1224 FOR X = 1 TO 60 :LPRINT "       adr(";X;") = ";AD(X) :NEXT X
1230    FOR Y = 1 TO 11
1240    PUB(Y) = 0   :  NPUB(Y) = 0
1250    NEXT Y
1260    FOR I = 1 TO 5
1270    FOR J = 1 TO 12
1280       X = ((I-1) * 12) + J
1290    IF AD(X) = 99 THEN 1380
1300    FOR Y = 1 TO 4
1310      NPUB(Y) = NPUB(Y) +  A(Y,J)
1320      NPUB(Y+4) = NPUB(Y+4) + (A(Y,J)*A(Y,J))
1330    NEXT Y
1340    IF A(3,J) = 6 THEN NPUB(9) = NPUB(9) + 1
1350    IF A(3,J) = 5 THEN NPUB(10) = NPUB(10) + 1
1360    IF A(3,J) = 4 THEN NPUB(11) = NPUB(11) + 1
1370       GOTO 1450
1380    FOR Y = 1 TO 4
1390      PUB(Y) = PUB(Y) +  A(Y,J)
1400      PUB(Y+4) = PUB(Y+4) + (A(Y,J)*A(Y,J))
```

(continued)

Table 7.3 (Continued)

```
1410    NEXT Y
1420    IF A(3,J) = 6 THEN PUB(9) = PUB(9) + 1
1430    IF A(3,J) = 5 THEN PUB(10) = PUB(10) + 1
1440    IF A(3,J) = 4 THEN PUB(11) = PUB(11) + 1
1450    NEXT J
1460    NEXT I
1465    FOR Y = 1 TO 11 :PRINT "pub(";Y;") =";PUB(Y) :NEXT Y
1466    FOR Y = 1 TO 11 :PRINT "npub(";Y;") =";NPUB(Y) :NEXT Y
1467    FOR Y = 1 TO 11 :LPRINT "pub(";Y;") =";PUB(Y) :NEXT Y
1468    FOR Y = 1 TO 11 :LPRINT "npub(";Y;") =";NPUB(Y) :NEXT Y
1470    FOR Y = 1 TO 4
1480    PUB(Y+4) =(PUB(Y+4) - ((PUB(Y)*PUB(Y))/10))/9
1483 PRINT "pub(y+4) = ";PUB(Y+4)
1484 LPRINT "pub(y+4) = ";PUB(Y+4)
1485    PUB(Y+4) = SQR(PUB(Y+4))
1490    PUB(Y) = PUB(Y)/10
1491 PRINT "npub(y+4) = ";NPUB(Y+4)
1492 LPRINT "npub(y+4) = ";NPUB(Y+4)
1500    NPUB(Y+4) =(NPUB(Y+4) - ((NPUB(Y)*NPUB(Y))/50))/49
1505    NPUB(Y+4) = SQR(NPUB(Y+4))
1510    NPUB(Y) = NPUB(Y)/50
1520    NEXT Y
1521 FOR Y=1 TO 3
1522    PUB(Y+8) = PUB(Y+8)/10
1523    NPUB(Y+8) = NPUB(Y+8)/50
1524    NEXT Y
1530    TN = TN + 1
1535 PRINT " TN = ";TN
1540    F1$=" ### # # # #   ##.## ##.## ##.## ##.##
1550    PRINT#1,USING F1$;TN,RS,RQ,EF,EP,PUB(1),PUB(2),PUB(3),PUB(4)
1551    PRINT,USING F1$;TN,RS,RQ,EF,EP,PUB(1),PUB(2),PUB(3),PUB(4)
1552 LPRINT,USING F1$;TN,RS,RQ,EF,EP,PUB(1),PUB(2),PUB(3),PUB(4)
1560    F2$=" ###           ##.## ##.## ##.## ##.##  #.##  #.##  #.##
1570    PRINT#1,USING F2$;TN,PUB(5),PUB(6),PUB(7),PUB(8),PUB(9),PUB(10),PUB(11)
1571    PRINT,USING F2$;TN,PUB(5),PUB(6),PUB(7),PUB(8),PUB(9),PUB(10),PUB(11)
1572 LPRINT,USING F2$;TN,PUB(5),PUB(6),PUB(7),PUB(8),PUB(9),PUB(10),PUB(11)
1580    PRINT#1,USING F1$;TN,RS,RQ,EF,EP,NPUB(1),NPUB(2),NPUB(3),NPUB(4)
1581    PRINT,USING F1$;TN,RS,RQ,EF,EP,NPUB(1),NPUB(2),NPUB(3),NPUB(4)
1582 LPRINT,USING F1$;TN,RS,RQ,EF,EP,NPUB(1),NPUB(2),NPUB(3),NPUB(4)
1590 PRINT#1,USING
F2$;TN,NPUB(5),NPUB(6),NPUB(7),NPUB(8),NPUB(9),NPUB(10),NPUB(11)
1591 PRINT,USING
F2$;TN,NPUB(5),NPUB(6),NPUB(7),NPUB(8),NPUB(9),NPUB(10),NPUB(11)
1592 LPRINT,USING
F2$;TN,NPUB(5),NPUB(6),NPUB(7),NPUB(8),NPUB(9),NPUB(10),NPUB(11)
1600 NEXT EP
1610 NEXT EF
1620 NEXT RQ
1630 NEXT RS
1640 CLOSE#1
1650    END
```

Table 7.4

Characteristics of Published and Unpublished Manuscripts

Quarterly Mean of Each Manuscript Characteristic (N = 120)	All Published Manuscripts	All Unpublished Manuscripts
Mean quality rating*	3.93	3.41
S.D., quality rating*	1.10	1.38
Mean author's prestige*	3.73	3.46
S.D., author's prestige*	1.10	1.38
Mean manuscript interest*	3.89	3.42
S.D., manuscript interest	1.30	1.35
Mean manuscript conventionality*	4.48	3.31
S.D., manuscript conventionality*	.90	1.34

NOTE: *A t-test for the difference between published and unpublished manuscripts establishes a statistically significant difference at $p < .05$.

conventionality per se that accounts for the gap in treatment of conventional versus unconventional manuscripts.

Finally, Table 7.4 also indicates that on every measure employed here, rejected manuscripts are at least as variable, and in most instances significantly more variable, than accepted ones. With regard to quality, the greater variability of rejected manuscripts reflects the low probability that a very weak manuscript will be published—a result for which a review process hardly can be faulted. With regard to conventionality and prestige, however, the relative homogeneity of the accepted manuscripts indicates that published articles are representative of the full range of submissions in ways that have nothing directly to do with merit.

What does the simulation suggest about the impacts of the three manipulated variables—the distribution of reviewer conventionality, the weight the editor places on the author's prestige, and the editor's openness to work distant from her own? Four separate $3 \times 2 \times 2$ analyses of variance (one for each quality and diversity measure) reveal that the distribution of reviewer conventionality has no significant effects whatsoever, nor is it involved in any significant interactions with the other two variables. On the other hand, both of the other manipulated variables significantly affect article quality and diversity. The full analysis of variance results are shown in Table 7.5 and the impacts of the two variables that matter are displayed graphically in Table 7.6.

Table 7.5
Analysis of Variance Summary

Source of Variation	Mean Quality	S.D. Quality	S.D. Prestige	S.D. Conventionality
		F-Ratio for:		
Conventionality	.39	.12	.51	1.59
Deference	1.18	13.56*	10.64*	42.94*
Openness	14.33*	11.50*	32.55*	58.60*
Conventionality × deference	.06	.51	.16	.11
Conventionality × openness	.01	.04	.66	.16
Deference × openness	5.65*	13.41*	2.91	36.26*
Conventionality × deference × openness	.41	.50	.21	.39
Eta squared	.18	.27	.31	.57

NOTE: *$p < .05$. The treatment variables are as follows: "Conventionality" = distribution of reviewer conventionality; "Prestige" = editor's deference to author's prestige; "Openness" = editor's openness to manuscripts of no interest to her.

According to Table 7.5, editorial openness significantly affects the quality of published articles, and there is also a significant interaction between openness and editorial deference. Table 7.6 (Part A), supplemented by standard follow-up tests, helps unravel these effects. A journal issue produced by a more open editor contains significantly better articles than an issue produced by her narrower counterpart. When the editor takes an author's prestige into account, however, her degree of openness has no significant bearing on the quality of the manuscripts she accepts; it is only when the editor pays no attention to prestige that openness matters. So the editor's openness has no *overall* effect on article quality, but when the author's prestige plays no part in the editor's calculations, the editor's openness does yield better articles for the journal.

A similar finding holds for the diversity of article quality under various types of editors (see Table 7.5 and Part B of Table 7.6). Although the main effects of both editor characteristics are significant, Table 7.6 (Part B) suggests, and follow-up tests confirm, that these main effects must be interpreted in light of a very strong interaction effect. An editor's degree of openness and her attentiveness to prestige have no impact on the range of quality in accepted articles except when she is simultaneously inattentive to prestige and biased against manuscripts in which she is personally interested. This, of course, is also the most

Table 7.6

Quality and Diversity Means by Deference and Openness

		Part A					Part B	
		Deference					Deference	
		Low	High				Low	High
Openness	High	4.22	4.07		Openness	High	.96	.96
	Low	3.52	3.91			Low	1.55	.94

Each entry in Part A is the mean of all the means in the cell (article quality). Each entry in Part B is the mean of all the standard deviations in the cell (article quality).

		Part C					Part D	
		Deference					Deference	
		Low	High				Low	High
Openness	High	.99	.90		Openness	High	.62	.70
	Low	1.44	1.14			Low	1.42	.87

Each entry in Part C is the mean of all the standard deviations in the cell (author's prestige). Each entry in Part D is the mean of all the standard deviations in the cell (article conventionality).

problematic combination of editorial characteristics as far as the mean quality of published manuscripts is concerned (see Part A of Table 7.6), so we can conclude that the quality of articles is both significantly lower and more variable when the review process is run by a narrow, non-deferential editor than under any other type of editor.

It should occasion no great surprise that the mean author's prestige score for accepted manuscripts varies significantly as a function of the weight the editor places on prestige (mean = 3.4 for non-prestige-oriented editors, 4.1 for prestige-oriented editors, $p < .05$); the editor's openness, on the other hand, has no significant effect. What is more interesting is that, as Tables 7.5 and 7.6 reveal, variability in the prestige of the authors of accepted articles is significantly linked to both the editor's concern about prestige and her openness. A concern on the editor's part with either of these factors significantly lessens variability in the prestige of published authors; that is, both these biases homogenize the journal by making it less representative of authors at a wide range of different levels in the academic stratification system.

The editor's predilections also significantly affect the conventionality of published articles. An editor unconcerned about prestige who favors manuscripts that are close to her own interests accepts manuscripts that are significantly less conventional. The explanation seems to be that by according preferential treatment to manuscripts whose topic she finds interesting, the editor often overrides low evaluations of the manuscript from reviewers who are put off by unconventionality; but the same effect does not consistently hold when the editor also is concerned about prestige, because the editor's two biases often offset one another. More important, the variability in article conventionality follows a similar pattern (see Table 7.5 and Part D of Table 7.6). Irrespective of any tendency to defer to prestigious authors, the editor who gives special weight to her own interests increases diversity in the conventionality or unconventionality of the manuscripts she accepts. The effect of the editor's emphasis on prestige, however, does not carry across the two openness conditions, because deference matters only for an editor who is biased against manuscripts she considers uninteresting. Again, it is the nondeferential, narrow editor who stands out; the variability in article conventionality for such an editor far outstrips the variability associated with any other experimental condition, apparently for the very same reason.

CONCLUSION

We believe that the simulation model faithfully represents the most essential elements of the peer review process, although the model obviously does not capture every component of the review process. Thus, while the simulation results obviously cannot be taken as literal descriptions of an actual peer review system, if the assumptions underlying the model are credible and the algorithms plausible, these results should at least point in the right general direction.

The simulation results point to the editor's crucial role in determining the quality and diversity of articles published in the journal. These results must be seen in the context of our initial assumption that the editor for the most part rather passively confines herself to selecting reviewers, reading reviews, and then mechanically generating decisions based directly upon the reviews. Even the editor who is swayed by considerations outside the reviews, such as an author's prestige or lack thereof, does not accept or reject manuscripts on that basis alone.

Rather, she factors prestige into her thinking alongside the reviewers' evaluations, which outweigh prestige by a 3:1 ratio. So her decision calculus is not "I respect the author of this manuscript, and will therefore accept the manuscript"; rather, it might be stated "Because I respect this scholar, I suspect that her manuscript is somewhat better than the reviewers are telling me. I will therefore upgrade their evaluations a bit." Such upgrading (or downgrading, in the case of a low-prestige author), can move a manuscript into (or out of) the circle of the charmed one-sixth that are published, but not unless there is a sizable gap between the reviewers' evaluations, on the one hand, and the author's prestige, on the other. The point is that the editor in the simulation is no autocrat who arbitrarily seals a manuscript's fate through her personal whims. In this light, it is especially striking that the simulation results highlight the impact that even a relatively passive editor can have on the quality and diversity of published articles.

We hasten to add that the validity of these conclusions depends, as always, upon the validity of our representation of the underlying process. If our assumptions or algorithms are basically flawed, then the conclusions we have derived will have no standing. If, however, our representation of the peer review process seems essentially reasonable, then our conclusions about the impact of bias in peer review should add a more systematic element than has previously been available to the often heated discussions of this important process.

8

The Art and Science of Simulation

Earlier in this book we described computer simulation as a mixture of art and science. This chapter concludes our introduction to computer simulation by identifying when the artistic aspects are more powerful, versus when scientific principles and techniques predominate.

How does art differ from science? Let us concede at the outset that there are great areas of overlap. That is, the stereotype of the cold, objective scientist is greatly overdrawn, and so is the stereotype of the wild, undisciplined artist. Still, there are differences.

Artistic beauty truly does lie in the eye of the beholder. Different people view artistic objects differently, depending upon their experience, prior exposure to the subject matter, and general aesthetic orientations and preferences. In art, there is only rarely a "right" or a "wrong" way to achieve beauty. Rather, there are more traditional and less traditional approaches, and there are competing schools of thought. Relativism takes precedence over the rigor of a rigid formula.

Science operates on the basis of established principles that guide process and procedure. In science, while there are often "judgment calls" that require the researcher to rely upon his or her experience and values, it is not unusual for there to be a right way and a wrong way to do things. Personal preferences are secondary to accepted principles and procedures. Rigor takes precedence over subjectivity.

In computer simulation, the reasons for building simulation models are predominantly scientific, but the actual building of the models combines science and art.

WHY USE SIMULATION MODELS?

We noted earlier that computer simulation modeling represents the nexus of three types of research activity: modeling (representing real-world phenomena in symbolic terms); simulation (the exploration of the impacts of various factors in a symbolic or hypothetical context); and the use of the computer as a research tool. As the nexus of these approaches, computer simulation modeling combines many of the powerful features of each.

Simulation is common in the physical and biological sciences. While its use has been more limited in the social sciences, it is spreading as more social scientists become aware of its power.

Simulation is a powerful theory building tool, allowing researchers to explore the linkages and interactions among theoretically interesting variables. Through sensitivity testing, simulation also is a powerful tool for restrospective, contemporary, or prospective policy testing, facilitating the systematic exploration of policies that have not yet been implemented or for which empirical data are scarce.

Computer simulation is a rigorous yet extremely flexible approach, allowing quantitative methods to be juxtaposed with researcher-determined assumptions and with conditions identified to fit specific situations. It approximates an experimental research design, and allows the researcher to control, by setting parameters, other forces that may affect the phenomena being studied. In contrast to empirical research, where typically only one set, or perhaps a limited set, of combinations of independent variable values can be explored, simulation facilitates the examination of a full set of independent variable values. This increases the power of simulation as a theory building tool.

Moreover, simulation is relatively inexpensive, compared to other forms of research activity, since it relies primarily upon the researcher's skill and imagination. It allows worst-case scenarios (e.g., the survivability of a nuclear attack) to be explored without really suffering the worst-case conditions. It also facilitates the exploration and identification of optimizing strategies and input conditions.

Thus understood, computer simulation is undertaken primarily for scientific reasons. The art of simulation enters in the construction phase.

HOW ARE SIMULATION MODELS BUILT AND USED?

Components of a Simulation Model

Simulation models have five fundamental components: assumptions (the researcher-specified conditions that underlie the model); inputs (the independent variables); parameters (the control variables); algorithms (the specific rules that convert input values into outputs); and outputs (the dependent variables).

These components are standard. All scientific work, for example, makes use of independent variables and dependent variables, and attempts, in some fashion, to hold other relevant factors constant. Similarly, assumptions are an inescapable part of scientific work, even if they are not always explicitly stated or even recognized. For example, researchers who employ standard regression techniques to analyze relationships between independent and dependent variables make certain assumptions about distributional qualities, error terms, linearity, and so on, because these assumptions are embodied in the technique. Critics sometimes charge that simulation relies too heavily upon assumptions, but in many cases what makes simulation stand out is simply that assumptions are more explicitly stated than critics are accustomed to seeing.

Even though the components are standard, their identification and specification involve a great deal of artistic creativity. Indeed, simulation demands a great deal more creativity than a normal scientific experiment or survey, for the modeler is not limited by data or by constraints of implementation, as is the empirical scientist. In this sense, simulation provides a means of systematizing the researcher's imagination, of asking "What if?" within an orderly framework.

To build a computer simulation model, researchers must identify the unit of analysis; the five components of the model (assumptions, inputs, parameters, algorithms, and outputs); the independent variable levels or values to be tested; and the time frame or number of periods over which the model will run. Here again, the task is a blend of science and art.

Since the simulation-based researcher is not constrained by real-world data limitations, he or she is free to model units for which real-world experiments are impossible. Thus liberated, the researcher is free to create models of the creation or expansion of the universe, or black holes or subatomic particles. The researcher also is free to specify extreme values of independent variables—more extreme values, if he or she wishes, than might be expected to occur in a normal set of observations—or unusual combinations of independent variable values. Similarly, the empirically based scientist must deal in real time, but the simulation-based researcher, like an artist, can ignore time boundaries and create, in effect, a timeless world.

Stochastic and Deterministic Models

A basic decision in any simulation is whether to make a model stochastic, in which case it includes probabilities that affect the disposition of each case tested, or deterministic, in which case it involves no probabilities that affect the outcome of each case. This decision, in turn, affects the number of runs that must be conducted in the simulation; the type of statistical tests that are applied to the output; and the certainty with which results can be stated.

If the model is stochastic, multiple runs must be conducted for each combination of the independent variable values. Because the results of these runs will vary, reflecting the presence of the stochastic element, output often is analyzed by an inferential statistical technique (e.g., analysis of variance), which permits the researcher to use randomly generated observations as a basis for generalizations about the underlying population of cases. In such instances, generalizations must be stated tentatively, in probabilistic terms, since, given random variation, there is no absolute certainty that a particular combination of conditions will produce a particular outcome.

If, on the other hand, the model is deterministic, only one run needs to be conducted for each combination of independent variable values. In that event, output analyses are apt to be simpler, consisting of straightforward reports of single output values or of descriptive statistics such as means and variances. Moreover, conclusions can be stated more firmly, without resort to probabilistic terms.

Generally, deterministic models, especially those that test all possible combinations of input variable values, are preferable to stochastic models, unless one has strong reasons for modeling uncertainty and including stochastic variation.

Making a model either stochastic or deterministic probably involves more science than art, since either the phenomenon being modeled obviously incorporates probabilities and stochastic error, or it does not. Even so, some phenomena are ambiguous, and the extent of stochastic variation depends, in part, upon the unit of analysis, which is a question of art as well as science. For example, modeling electoral behavior at the level of whole nations might involve a deterministic model vacillating between left- and right-wing political ideologies, while modeling electoral behavior at the individual level might involve a probabilistic approach.

Determining the number of runs and settling other tactical issues, once the basic decision has been made between probabilistic and deterministic approaches, tends to involve established algorithms, or at least rules of thumb; to this extent we would characterize it as more scientific than artistic.

Programming Languages

Once a model is designed, the researcher must decide whether to program it with a general-purpose language, such as BASIC or FORTRAN, or a specialized simulation language, such as SIMSCRIPT or HOCUS. General-purpose languages are more readily available and better supported, while specialized simulation languages often have useful initializing, collecting, and reporting functions.

Deciding which computer language to use is, among other things, a matter of artistic taste, as a wide array of languages can accommodate many simulation models. The situation facing the modeler, then, is in this sense much like that facing an artist, who has a choice of whether to paint in oils, acrylics, or watercolors, or, for that matter, to use chalk, charcoal, or another medium instead of paint.

Programming Habits

Good programming habits involve extensive documentation; modular programming, when possible; debugging programming sections; and hand tracing single examples to test for logical errors. These are largely techniques that can be learned and applied systematically. As matters of technique, they neither are inherently scientific nor inherently artistic, since technical skills are vital for success in both science and art. As is true of any skill, some people have greater technical aptitude than others, but learning the basics of good programming habits is easily within the reach of the beginner.

Validation and Verification

Depending on the subject matter being simulated, varying degrees o verification and validation can be obtained, including establishing face validity (the reasonableness of the model among practitioners or scholars expert in the field); validating model assumptions (through the use of prior studies or the collection of data); and comparing model input-output transformations to real-world input-output transformations (the most difficult level of validation and one rarely achieved).

Validation and verification involve an element of creativity in generating, locating, and using appropriate data sets, but this is largely scientific creativity, similar to the creativity a good empirical scientist uses in collecting data to analyze a problem.

WHAT ARE THE LIMITATIONS OF COMPUTER SIMULATION MODELING?

We would point to three major potential limitations of computer simulation modeling.

First, simulation is not a substitute for empirical research, but a complement to it. Simulation fills a need in theory building and policy analysis that empirical research cannot meet when empirical data cannot be summoned to analyze the problem under consideration.

Second, simulation results are highly dependent upon the assumptions made and the initializing values of the independent variables. Fortunately, any potential biases can be explored by changing either or both.

Finally, simulation models and results can be difficult to convey to novices, who tend either to be overawed by the complexity and sheer volume of numbers generated, or to be hypercritical of the assumptions made. By comparison, the limiting assumptions made in traditional empirical research are rarely laid out explicitly for criticism.

WHAT DO RESEARCHERS NEED IN ORDER TO CONDUCT SIMULATIONS?

Researchers interested in building simulation models and exploring relationships, linkages, and interactions through sensitivity testing need a number of different skills, including the following:

- familiarity with the problem being modeled;
- an awareness of the logic and constraints involved in computer programming and, preferably, an ability to write computer programs;

- familiarity with basic research design concepts and issues, especially those dealing with experimental research design;
- familiarity with basic procedures for statistical data analysis, particularly analysis of variance and other techniques appropriate for data drawn from experimental designs; and
- an awareness of the capacities and limitations of various types of computers, compilers, and operating systems.

Additionally, several personal characteristics are useful for the simulation modeler:

- an ability to think through processes logically;
- a capacity for dealing with both the theoretical level of concepts and design, and with the operational level of variable values and programming detail, as the decisions that are made at each level affect the results and the utility of the modeling exercise;
- an ability to abstract out the central elements of a problem, identifying the major issues while laying less significant factors aside;
- creativity and imagination; and
- extreme patience and persistence. Good simulation models, like Rome, are not built in a single day. Rather, successful modeling is a matter of successive approximations.

WHERE DO YOU GO FROM HERE?

A central part of the skill in developing useful simulation models lies in defining a problem that lends itself to the approach, just as a central part of writing a good doctoral dissertation lies in specifying a reasonable dissertation topic. Experienced dissertation advisors know that good dissertation topics speak to a theoretically interesting set of questions without trying to answer all the world's unanswered questions; focus on clearly defined, testable hypotheses; contain variables that are amenable to measurement; and are "doable" within a reasonable period of time. The problems that lend themselves most readily to a simulation-based approach share all of these characteristics, and possess two more as well.

First, they cannot be approached purely through mathematical techniques, because it may not be obvious which type of mathematics is applicable, or because available mathematical techniques may contain restrictive assumptions that render them inapplicable to the problem a hand, or because the difficulty of attempting mathematical proofs is so great that simulation is more feasible.

Second, they cannot be approached via standard empirical data-collection techniques because they ask questions about a policy or option that has only been proposed and not yet adopted, or because one or more of the phenomena of interest is not currently measurable, or because there is no way in the real world to impose the needed experimental controls.

The range of "simulable" problems is limited only by the researcher's imagination and skills. A social psychologist might develop a simulation to explore the impact of various residential and familial arrangements on crowding-linked aggression. An economist might develop a simulation to gain a clearer perspective on the combination of tax laws, infrastructure allocations, and export efforts most conducive to economic growth. A sociologist might develop a simulation to probe the effects of different promotion criteria, organizational structures, and level of centralization upon the differential advancement of men and women to positions of authority. A political scientist might develop a simulation to project the impact of a federal, unitary, or mixed governmental structure on the outputs of a new government jurisdiction. And a demographer might develop a simulation to clarify the short- and long-term effects of various birth control technologies on the size and age characteristics of the population. These hardly are trivial problems, nor are countless others from various fields of inquiry; all of which are difficult to examine using conventional tools of analysis but are potentially simulable.

A Selected Annotated Bibliography on Computer Simulation Modeling

This book presents an introductory overview of computer simulation applications in the social sciences. It does not pretend to be an exhaustive treatment of the subject. Those with a serious interest in computer simulation modeling should definitely consult other sources—many of them much more technical—before striking out on their own. This bibliography is intended to be of use to such readers. The bibliography presents an annotated list of books on various aspects of computer simulation modeling, along with a list of relevant journal articles.

BOOKS

Many current treatments of simulation discuss simulations designed for teaching, skill development by users, or classroom use rather than the use of computer simulation modeling as a tool for theory development and policy analysis. Works in the latter vein typically are not aimed toward social scientists, but rather are designed for audiences in mathematics, computer science, engineering, instrumentation, and the physical sciences. The following is a partial listing of some of these books, primarily from fields other than the social sciences, which explore or illustrate the use of simulation. Many are highly technical and may not be accessible to the average social scientist.

Adam, N. R., and A. Dogramaci (eds.). 1979. *Current Issues on Computer Simulation.* New York: Academic Press.

> In the first part of this book, contributors discuss the advantages and disadvantages of several simulation languages. The second part presents an overview of applications of computer simulation modeling in a variety of areas. In the third part, the statistical aspects of simulation and linkages to analytic models are explored.

Barton, R. F. 1970. *A Primer on Simulation and Gaming.* Englewood Cliffs, NJ: Prentice-Hall.

Basic topics in simulation are discussed in nonmathematical, nonprogramming-oriented language. Programs are illustrated with flow diagrams or examples. Applications are derived from business, administration, and data processing. Techniques of analysis, person-model, simulation, person-computer simulation, and all-computer simulation are illustrated, and Monte Carlo techniques, simulation languages, and a variety of simulation applications are discussed.

Bloom, P. N. 1976. *Advertising, Competition, and Public Policy: A Simulation Study.* Cambridge, MA: Ballinger.

This book develops a computer simulation model to test the implications of various proposals by economists, consumer advocates, and others who consider advertising potentially anticompetitive and who believe certain industries would become more competitive if their firms were required or encouraged to modify their advertising budgets. Experiments conducted with the model explore the competitive effects of seven proposed advertising reforms.

Boden, M. A. 1988. *Computer Models of the Mind: Computational Approaches in Theoretical Psychology.* New York: Cambridge University Press.

Nonmathematical in approach, this book asks how computer models have been used and might be used to assist in formulating theories of the mind. Models are chosen for their psychological significance, not their technical promise. Topics include imagery in experiment and theory, connectionist models of vision, natural language, meaning and messages, reasoning and rationality, and learning and development.

Bratley, P., B. L. Fox, and L. E. Schrage. 1983. *A Guide to Simulation.* New York: Springer-Verlag.

These authors contend that many simulations are statistically defective and many simulation programs are inefficient. They emphasize effective simulation in their discussion of the three crucial components of any simulation project: (1) data gathering, model building, and validation; (2) statistical design and estimation; and (3) programming and implementation. They cover program verification; approximation and validation; clock mechanisms; hints for simulation programming; analysis of steady-state performance through batch regenerative, spectral analysis, and autoregressive methods; analysis of transaction-based performance; efficiency of estimators; statistical distributions for number generation; simulation with general-purpose languages; several specific simulation languages; and programming to reduce variance.

Brier, A., and I. Robinson. 1974. *Computers and the Social Sciences*. New York: Columbia University Press.

The entire range of computer applications to the social sciences is the focus. One chapter deals specifically with computer simulation, and includes a discussion of models using transition probabilities such as Markov models, models of continuous dynamic processes, human-machine simulations, and behavior simulation and artificial intelligence.

Bulgren, W. G. 1982. *Discrete System Simulation*. Englewood Cliffs, NJ: Prentice-Hall.

Tools for learning discrete system simulation, including statistics, simulation languages, elementary queuing theory, advanced programming techniques, random number and random variable generation, and elementary modeling techniques are presented.

Cellier, F. E. (ed.). 1982. *Progress in Modelling and Simulation*. New York: Academic Press.

This edited volume reports on progress in simulation through the early 1980s. Topics include ill-defined system modeling, large-scale system modeling, experimentation with models, and graphical techniques in modeling.

Condon, A. 1989. *Computational Models of Games*. Cambridge: MIT Press.

This volume (originally a doctoral thesis selected by the Association for Computing Machinery for its 1988 Distinguished Dissertation Award) develops a new model of two-person games.

Crecine, J. P. 1969. *Governmental Problem-Solving: A Computer Simulation of Municipal Budgeting*. Chicago: Rand McNally.

Now a classic in budgeting and political science, this book develops a simulation model to fit interview data collected from participants in the municipal budget process. Crecine incorporates substantive discussions of budgetary concepts and optimizing processes as well as methodological discussions of his research strategy, the development of his budget model, goodness-of-fit tests, and sensitivity analyses. The budget model includes three submodels that focus on budget strategies at the departmental, mayoral, and council levels. Model parameters and tests of the model are developed, using data from three cities.

Dyke, B., and J. W. MacCluer. 1974. *Computer Simulation in Human Population Studies*. New York: Academic Press.

This book discusses the growing emphasis in anthropology, demography, and human population genetics upon computer simulation models of human populations. Because simulation models usually are so complex that investigators cannot publish detailed accounts of simulation techniques, a number of similar problems have been encountered and independently solved or dismissed at considerable cost in time and effort. This volume addresses some of these common problems, and reports on simulation efforts in these fields.

Evans, J. B. 1988. *Structure of Discrete Event Simulation: An Introduction to the Engagement Strategy.* New York: John Wiley.

The author stresses the structural aspects of discrete-event simulation to address the linguistic problem of describing a dynamic system in formal terms that can be used to define a computer program. This book is highly readable by a novice.

Fishman, G. S. 1978. *Principles of Discrete Event Simulation.* New York: John Wiley.

This book includes a discussion of four simulation languages (SIMSCRIPT II.5, GPSS, SIMPL/1, and SIMULA), as well as the process interaction and time series approaches to output analysis, fixed time advance, nonstationarity, random number generation, and sampling on a computer with a large number of different distributions.

Gottfried, B. S. 1984. *Elements of Stochastic Process Simulation.* Englewood Cliffs, NJ: Prentice-Hall.

Developed as an introductory text on stochastic process simulation for business curricula, this book builds simulation concepts systematically, beginning with simple ideas of system components, uniformly distributed random variates, and nonuniform random variates, and developing industrial, business, and queuing applications and special-purpose simulation languages. Languages discussed include FORTRAN and BASIC as well as special-purpose simulation languages. Examples are provided in FORTRAN to convey insights into the logical intricacies of the models.

Graybeal, W. J., and U. W. Pooch. 1980. *Simulation: Principles and Methods.* Cambridge, MA: Winthrop.

Another introductory text on simulation suitable for undergraduate or beginning graduate students in engineering and computer science, this volume addresses the standard array of topics, including basic concepts and terminology, probability and distribution theory, estimation and statistical tests, generation of random numbers, queuing theory, discrete system simulation, languages for discrete system simulation, continuous system simulation, and the design of simulation experiments.

Hovanessian, S. A., and L. A. Pipes. 1969. *Digital Computer Methods in Engineering.* New York: McGraw-Hill.

This book contains introductory material on numerical methods of solving engineering problems by digital computers. The primary emphasis is on mathematical skill development rather than computer simulation. Topics include determinants, matrices, linear simultaneous equations, eigenvalues, eigenvectors, quadratic forms, roots of polynomial and algebraic equations, Lagrange's interpolation formula, least squares, time-frequency domain analyses, and fast Fourier transforms.

Ingels, D. M. 1985. *What Every Engineer Should Know About Computer Modeling and Simulation.* New York: Marcel Dekker.

Written as a springboard for beginning students in simulation, the book discusses the generation of mathematical models, including linear and nonlinear algebra systems, differential equations, stochastic systems, the characteristics of good software, documentation, software development and testing, data input, the preprocessing and calculation phases, and the output and analysis phases.

Korn, G. A., and J. V. Wait. 1978. *Digital Continuous-System Simulation.* Englewood Cliffs, NJ: Prentice-Hall.

Korn and Wait introduce digital computer techniques designed to free the user from programming details, including equation-oriented simulation languages, simple output commands to produce solution time histories, cross plots, listings, reports, and interactive minicomputer systems. The authors also include a discussion of equation-oriented, continuous-system simulation languages, proceeding from simple applications to advanced language features, function generation, and multirun studies.

Lehman, R. S. 1977. *Computer Simulation and Modeling: An Introduction.* Hillsdale, NJ: Lawrence Erlbaum.

This book is one of the few that applies simulation directly to the social sciences, drawing illustrations from psychology, sociology, and urban development. More accessible to the social science student than most books on simulation, the book discusses planning and organizing a simulation project, data requirements and structures, working with data structures, random processes, coding accuracy and efficiency, debugging, documentation, and validation. The primary focus is on the mechanics of simulation, although the author does discuss the reasons for simulation and the need to incorporate theory into simulation algorithms and programs.

Lewis, P.A.W., and E. J. Orav. 1989. *Simulation Methodology for Statisticians, Operations Analysts, and Engineers.* Pacific Grove, CA: Wadsworth and Brooks/Cole.

Assuming intermediate levels of mathematical skill and understanding of probability theory by the reader, this book covers the use of simulation methodology in both mathematical statistics and system simulation. Statistical methods based on graphical techniques and exploratory data analysis are covered.

Madisetti, V. (ed.). 1990. *Modeling and Simulation on Microcomputers, 1990*. San Diego: Society for Computer Simulation.

This volume covers an array of topics, including adding knowledge-based computing to LOTUS 1-2-3; a space station mobile servicing center real time simulator; a methodology for performance comparisons on UNIX microprocessors; the anatomy of rule-based simulation; and simulating labor resource allocations in large-scale projects.

Maryanski, F. 1980. *Digital Computer Simulation*. Rochelle Park, NJ: Hayden.

This book assumes experience with high-level programming language and some mathematical sophistication. Topics include an introduction to systems modeling; discrete system simulation, including the representation of time, the generation of event distributions, scheduling of events, queuing, multiqueue, and multiserver models; queuing statistics, and bias in queuing statistics. GPSS and SIMSCRIPT are introduced, and probability and statistics are discussed. The book concludes with a discussion of continuous simulation modeling programs.

McMillian, C., and R. F. Gonzalez. 1968. *Systems Analysis: A Computer Approach to Decision Models*. Homewood, IL: Richard D. Irwin.

This book proceeds from discussions of particular models to the general model, and from consideration of subsystems to the consideration of complex collections of subsystems. The computer language emphasized is FORTRAN. The book is oriented mostly toward business students, and the concluding chapters deal with large-scale simulations of the firm.

Meyer, H. I., and M. C. Weaver. 1977. *Corporate Financial Planning Models*. New York: John Wiley.

The authors argue that the installation of an ongoing forecasting and planning model in the corporation is crucial and describe how it is done, from convincing key people of its need to choosing the appropriate software, data input, and report generation.

Mihram, G. A. 1972. *Simulation: Statistical Foundations and Methodology*. New York: Academic Press.

Mihram argues that the systems approach is firmly embedded in practically every discipline that endeavors to explain or predict observable phenomena. The essence of the systems approach is modeling. This text covers a broad range of topics related to modeling, spanning Monte Carlo techniques, queues, model development, verification, validation, and analysis, experimental designs, optimal system conditions, and simulation as a stochastic process.

Naylor, T. H. (ed.). 1969. *The Design of Computer Simulation Experiments*. Durham, NC: Duke University Press.

This collection covers experimental designs, data analysis, and other methodological problems associated with computer simulation modeling. Four designs are included: experimental designs, factor selection, response surface designs, and sequential designs. Data analysis and other methodological topics include regression and analysis of variance, selection and ranking procedures, times series, Monte Carlo techniques, and sampling. Examples are provided of economic policies, nonlinear economic models, complex organization processes, life insurance models, and risk theory models.

Orcutt, G., S. Caldwell, and R. Wertheimer II. 1976. *Policy Exploration Through Microanalytic Simulation*. Washington, DC: The Urban Institute.

This book describes a model developed by the Urban Institute to address national policy questions. The model starts with a representative sample of individuals and families, incorporating their differences in age, education, race, sex, work experience, welfare benefits, and so on. Using knowledge concerning behavioral development, it ages the individuals from year to year so they experience marriages and divorces, give birth, become unemployed, find new jobs, change residences, and die. Each year's simulation is based on output from the prior year's simulation.

Oren, T. I., B. P. Zeigler, and M. S. Elzas (eds.). 1982. *Simulation and Model-Based Methodologies: An Integrative View*. NATO ASI Series F: Computer and System Sciences (Vol. 10). New York: Springer-Verlag.

The book consists of six sections: (1) the conceptual basis for system modeling and design; (2) model-based simulation architecture; (3) the impact of formalism on model formulation; (4) model identification, reconstruction, and optimization; (5) quality assurance in model-based activities; and (6) workshop presentations.

Pidd, M. (ed.). 1989. *Computer Modelling for Discrete Simulation*. New York: John Wiley.

Focusing on the production of working simulations with a reasonable time scale, Pidd and other contributors examine developments in discrete simulation, the implementation of simulation languages, simulation support environments, graphics and interaction, and the nexus of simulation with artificial intelligence.

Reklaitis, G. V., A. Ravindran, and K. M. Ragsdell. 1983. *Engineering Optimization: Methods and Applications*. New York: John Wiley.

This is a text on the practical applications of optimization methodology, with a major focus on techniques and strategies relevant to engineering applications concerned with system design, operations, and analysis.

Shannon, R. E. 1975. *Systems Simulation: The Art and Science*. Englewood Cliffs, NJ: Prentice-Hall.

Criteria for model specification, experimentation and sensitivity analysis, tactical planning, the use of Tchebycheff's Theorem, determination of sample size, autocorrelated data, the use of automatic stopping rules, variance reduction techniques, importance sampling, Russian roulette and splitting, and antithetic variates are some of the topics in this introduction to system simulation. Shannon's discussion of validation and analysis includes subjective versus objective methods, rationalist versus empiricist tensions, absolute pragmatic versus utilitarian approaches, tests of internal structure and hypotheses, comparison of input-output transformations, the multiple response problem, and field tests.

Shapiro, G., and M. Rogers. 1967. *Prospects for Simulation and Simulators of Dynamic Systems*. New York: Spartan.

User-oriented papers discuss problems that can be solved only by simulation in the fields of atmospheric circulation, aeroelasticity, statistical mechanics, biophysics, biological mechanisms, as well as combinatorial, nonquantitative, control, human-machine, and interdisciplinary problems. Supplier-oriented papers discuss both hardware and software issues, including addressable memories, nonnumerical machines, hybrids, and human-machine combinations and systems that recognize unusual events or data trends. Now dated, this book provides insight into how much simulation has developed in the subsequent decades.

Spriet, J. A., and G. C. Vansteenkiste. 1982. *Computer-Aided Modeling and Simulation*. New York: Academic Press.

Modeling topics include mathematical models, model-building methodology for difference, differential, and partial differential equations, and methodology for model information storage and integration. Support languages for model simulation, hardware trends and their impact upon simulation, and simulation systems and architectures also are explored.

Tucker, A. B. 1986. *Programming Languages* (2nd ed.). New York: McGraw-Hill.

Although it does not directly address simulations, this book provides an excellent overview of the applications of programming languages for scientific purposes, data processing, text processing, artificial intelligence, and systems programming, as well as separate chapters on language syntax and semantics. Languages covered are PASCAL, FORTRAN, COBOL, PL/1, SNOBOL, APL, LISP, PROLOG, C, ADA, and MODULA-2.

Watson, H. J. 1981. *Computer Simulation in Business.* New York: John Wiley.

Written for a business administration audience, this volume discusses simulation in a largely programming-independent manner. When examples include programming code, FORTRAN is used. Standard simulation topics are covered.

Widman, L. E., K. A. Loparo, and N. R. Nielson. 1989. *Artificial Intelligence, Simulation, and Modeling.* New York: John Wiley.

This volume examines the relationship between artificial intelligence and computer simulation from two perspectives: that of traditional simulationists seeking the greater representational flexibility and ease of use that AI techniques can provide, and that of computer scientists seeking the greater power and realism that rigorous simulation techniques can provide. The three parts of the book deal with the theoretical underpinnings of AI and simulation, the application of simulation techniques to current research problems in AI, and the application of AI methods to the needs of simulationists and simulation users.

Zeigler, B. P. 1976. *Theory of Modeling and Simulation.* New York: John Wiley.

The first part of this book includes an interesting, though now dated, discussion of the use of simulations and models, while the second part, oriented toward computer science students, discusses aspects of model development, including the hierarchy of system specifications, the hierarchy of preservation relations, approximation and error toleration, and state identification, validation, and prediction.

Zeigler, B. P., M. S. Elzas, G. J. Klir, and T. I. Oren (eds.). 1979. *Methodology in Systems Modeling and Simulation.* New York: North-Holland.

This book defines modeling and simulation, explores future directions for methodological development, and reviews selected works relevant to the methodology for readers wishing to acquire a broader perspective. Articles range from multifaceted models, including strategies for standardization in socioeconomic models and integrated modeling applied to energy systems, to the software concerns of interactive simulation program generation, hierarchical and self-structuring simulation systems, and combined continuous/discrete system simulation languages. One article deals specifically with probabilistic constraints and structural identification involved in social science applications.

ARTICLES

"A Newly Modeled World." 1984. *Economist* 292 (August 11): 80.

Anderson, P. A., and S. J. Thompson. 1982. "Artificial Intelligence Based Simulations of Foreign Policy Decision-Making." *Behavioral Scientist* 27 (April): 176-193.

Barton, R. F. 1980. "Creating and Controlling Simulated Industries for Verisimilitude." *Simulation and Games* 11 (December): 441-450.

Berven, N. L. 1985. "Reliability and Validity of Standardized Case Management Simulations." *Journal of Counseling Psychology* 32 (July): 397-409.

Blackman, S. 1985. "Comparisons Among Methods of Scoring Androgyny Continuously Using Computer-Simulated Data." *Psychological Reports* 57 (August): 151-154.

Cohen, M. D. 1984. "Conflict and Complexity: Goal Diversity and Organizational Search Effectiveness." *American Political Science Review* 78 (June): 435-451.

Cole, R. L., and S. J. Wayne. 1980. "Predicting Presidential Decisions on Enrolled Bills: A Computer Simulation." *Simulation and Games* 11 (September): 313-325.

Culp, G. H., L. N. Seever, and B. Davidson. 1980. "INS2: Inter-nation Simulation." *Simulation and Games* 11 (December): 485-489.

Denker, M. W., *et al.* 1986. "Computer Simulation of Freud's Counterwill Theory: Extension to Elementary Social Behavior." *Behavioral Scientist* 31 (April): 103-141.

Dometrius, N. C., and L. Sigelman. 1988. "The Cost of Quality: Teacher Testing and Racial/Ethnic Representativeness in Public Education." *Social Science Quarterly* (March): 70-82.

Dometrius, N. C., and L. Sigelman. 1988. "Modeling the Impact of Supreme Court Decisions: *Wygant v. Board*." *Journal of Politics* (February): 131-149.

Grafton, C., and A. Permaloff. 1984. "Simulations and the Microcomputer." *PS* 17 (Summer): 698-706.

Hauck, W. W., and S. Anderson. 1984. "A Survey Regarding the Reporting of Simulation Studies." *American Statistics* 38 (August): 214-216.

Hubner-Dick, G., and R. Seidelmann. 1978. "Stimulating Economic Sanctions and Incentives: Hypothetical Alternatives of U.S. Policy on South Africa." *Journal of Peace Research* 15 (no. 2): 153-174.

Kleinmuntz, D. N., and B. Kleinmuntz. 1981. "System Simulation Decision Strategies in Simulated Environments." *Behavioral Science* 26 (July): 294-305.

Kramer, M. M. 1986. "The Use of Simulation in Political Science: Proven Technique or Passing Fad?" *Annual Review of Political Science* (vol. 1). Samuel Long (ed.). Norwood, NJ: Ablex.

Kroeck, K. G., *et al.* 1983. "Imposed Quotas and Personnel Selection." *Journal of Applied Psychology* 68 (February): 123-136.

Krus, O. J., and H. S. Blackman. 1980. "The Time-Scale Factor as Related to Theories of Societal Change." *Psychological Reports* 46 (February): 95-102.

Kunce, J. T., *et al.* 1981. "Interactional Personality, Mathematical Simulation, and Prediction of Interpersonal Compatibility." *Journal of Clinical Psychology* 37 (October): 749-754.

Law-Yone, H. 1982. "Games for Citizen Participation." *Simulation and Games* 13 (March): 51-62.

Min, F. B. M., and H. A. J. S. Boudier. 1985. "The RLCS System for Computer Simulation in Medical Education." *Simulation and Games* 16 (December): 429-440.

Muir, D. E. 1985. "A Mathematical Model/Computer Simulation of Adaptive System Interaction." *Behavioral Science* 31: 29-41.

Murphy, M. J. *et al.* 1982. "Simulating Collective Bargaining in Education." *Simulation and Games* 13 (June): 131-144.

Parker, R. *et al.* 1983. "Computer Laboratory for Studying Resource Dilemmas." *Behavioral Science* 28 (October): 298-304.

Penrod, S., and R. Hastie. 1980. "Computer Simulation of Jury Decision-Making." *Psychological Review* 87 (March): 133-159.

Pepin, M., *et al.* 1985. "Microcomputer Games and Sex Related Differences: Spatial, Verbal, and Mathematical Abilities." *Psychological Reports* 56 (June): 783-786.

Peterson, A. V., Jr., and R. A. Kronmal. 1982. "On Mixture Methods for the Computer Generation of Random Variables." *American Statistician* 36 (August, pt. 1): 184-191.

Pollins, B. M. 1985. "Breaking Trade Dependency: A Global Simulation of Third World Proposals for Alternative Trade Regimes." *International Studies Quarterly* 29 (September): 287-312.

Radin, D. I. 1985. "Pseudorandom Number Generators in Psi Research." *Journal of Parapsychology* 49 (December): 303-328.

Reither, F. 1981. "Thinking and Acting in Complex Situations: A Study of Experts' Behavior." *Simulation and Games* 12 (June): 125-140.

Roth, E. A. 1981. "Demography and Computer Simulation in Historic Village Population Reconstruction." *Journal of Anthropology Research* 37 (Fall): 279-301.

Rubin, H. J. 1981. "Applied Simulations and Persuasion Campaigns: Designs in Rural Villages." *Simulation and Games* 12 (March): 85-98.

Sigelman, L., and N. C. Dometrius. 1986. "Organizational Regeneration: A Model with Applications to Affirmative Action." *American Journal of Political Science* (February): 79-107.

Sigelman, L., and M. L. Whicker. 1987. "Some Implications of Bias in Peer Review: A Simulation-Based Analysis." *Social Science Quarterly* (September): 494-509.

Starbuck, W. H. 1983. "Computer Simulation of Human Behavior." *Behavioral Science* 28 (April): 154-165.

Stoll, R. J. 1983. "Nations at the Brink: A Computer Simulation of Governmental Behavior During Serious Disputes." *Simulation and Games* 14 (June): 179-200.

Tanford, S., and S. Penrod. 1983. "Computer Modeling of Influence in the Jury: The Role of the Consistent Juror." *Social Psychology Quarterly* 46 (September): 200-212.

Tanford, S., and S. Penrod. 1985. "Social Influence Model: A Formal Integration of Research on Majority and Minority Influence Processes." *Psychology Bulletin* 95 (March): 189-225.

Tsai, Y-m., O. Bartos, and L. Sigelman. 1981. "The Urban Dynamics Model: A Validation Study." *Urban Affairs Quarterly (December): 195-218.*

Valadez, J. J. 1983. "Global Systems Simulation: A Civil Servant Module for Multilocational Participation." *Simulation and Games* 14 (December): 417-428.

Wallace, C. M. 1982. "Reconstructing Traffic Accidents through the Eye of the Computer." *Trial* 18 (April): 24-27.

Watson, H. J., and D. P. Christy. 1982. "Evolving Use of Simulation." *Simulation and Games* 13 (September): 351-363.

Whicker, M. L. 1986. "Direct Democracy Devices: A Computer Simulation Analysis." *Journal of Policy Modeling* 8 (Summer): 255-272.

Whicker, M. L. 1986. "The Use of Deductive and Inductive Tools in the Study of Politics: A Comparison of Alternative Methodologies." *Southeastern Political Review* 14 (Spring): 201-218.

Whicker, M. L., and A. R. Mauet. 1983. "Computer Simulation Modeling: A Tool for Studying Organizations." *Administration and Society* 14 (February): 481-506.

Whicker, M. L., and R. A. Moore. 1985. "A Computer Simulation of Fiscal Restraints on the Congressional Budget Process." *Modeling and Simulation* (vol. 1): 15-19. Pittsburgh: University of Pittsburgh.

Wright, J. R., and A. S. Goldberg. 1985. "Risk and Uncertainty as Factors in the Durability of Political Conditions." *American Political Science Review* 79 (September): 704-718.

Yeager, R. F. 1979. "Rationality and Retrenchment: The Use of a Computer Simulation to Aid Decision-Making in School Closings." *Education and Urban Sociology* 11 (May): 296-312.

Zeigler, B. P. (symposium editor). 1984. "A Systems Approach to Investigating Interpersonal Strife." *Journal of Clinical Psychology* 40 (May): 713-716.

References

Abelson, R. P. 1981. "Going after PARRY." *Behavioral and Brain Sciences* 4: 534-535.

Ackoff, R. L., and M. W. Sasieni. 1968. *Fundamentals of Operations Research.* New York: John Wiley.

Apter, M. J. 1970. *The Computer Simulation of Behavior.* London: Hutchinson.

Banks, J., and J. S. Carson II. 1984. *Discrete-Event System Simulation.* Englewood Cliffs, NJ: Prentice-Hall.

Barton, R. F. 1970. *A Primer on Simulation and Gaming.* Englewood Cliffs, NJ: Prentice-Hall.

Bulgren, W. G. 1982. *Discrete System Simulation.* Englewood Cliffs, NJ: Prentice-Hall.

Colella, A. M., M. J. O'Sullivan, and D. J. Carlino. 1974. *Systems Simulation.* Lexington, MA: Lexington Books.

Cook, T. D., and D. T. Campbell. 1979. *Quasi-Experimentation: Design & Analysis Issues for Field Settings.* Chicago: Rand McNally.

Elzas, M. S. 1984. "System Paradigms as Reality Mappings." Pp. 41-60 in T. I. Oren, B. P. Zeigler, and M. S. Elzas (eds.), *Simulation and Model-Based Methodologies: An Integrative View.* New York: Springer Verlag.

Emshoff, J. R., and R. L. Sisson. 1970. *Design and Use of Computer Simulation Models.* New York: Macmillan.

Fishman, G. S. 1973. *Concepts and Methods in Discrete Event Digital Simulation.* New York: John Wiley.

Gerritsma, J.G.M., and K. A. Smal. 1987. "A Validation Strategy for a Complex Simulation of the Study of Medical Decision Making." *Simulation and Games* 18 (March): 35-56.

Gierce, R. N. 1988. *Explaining Science: A Cognitive Approach.* Chicago: University of Chicago Press.

Kaplan, A. 1964. *The Conduct of Inquiry.* New York: Chandler.

Lewin, K. 1975. *Field Theory in Social Science: Selected Theoretical Papers.* Westport, CT: Greenwood.

Lipsey, M. W. 1990. *Design Sensitivity: Statistical Power for Experimental Research.* Newbury Park, CA: Sage.

Little, J.D.C. 1970. "Models and Managers: The Concept of a Decision Calculus." *Management Science* 16 (April).

Meir, R. C., W. T. Newell, and H. L. Pazer. 1969. *Simulation in Business and Economics.* Englewood Cliffs, NJ: Prentice-Hall.

Mihram, G. A. 1972. *Simulation: Statistical Foundations and Methodology.* New York: Academic Press.

Moore, C. M. 1987. *Group Techniques for Idea Building.* Newbury Park, CA: Sage.

Morris, W. T. 1967. "On the Art of Modeling." *Management Science* 13 (August).

Norris, D. R., and C. A. Snyder. 1982. "External Validation of Simulation Games." *Simulation and Games* 13 (March): 73-84.

Petrinovich, L. 1979. "Probabilistic Functionalism." *American Psychologist* 34: 373-390.

Pidd, M. 1984. *Computer Simulation in Management Science.* New York: John Wiley.

Poole, T. G., and J. Z. Szymankiewicz. 1977. *Using Simulation to Solve Problems.* New York: McGraw-Hill.

Revlin, R. 1981. "Evaluation of a Model's Test." *Behavioral and Brain Sciences* 4: 547-548.

Shannon, R. E. 1975. *System Simulation: The Art and Science.* Englewood Cliffs, NJ: Prentice-Hall.

Sigelman, L., and M. L. Whicker. 1987. "Some Implications of Bias in Peer Review: A Simulation-Based Analysis." *Social Sciences Quarterly* (September): 494-509.

Stanislaw, H. 1986. "Tests of Computer Simulation Validity: What Do They Measure?" *Simulation and Games* 17 (June): 173-191.

Stoll, R. J. 1983. "Nations at the Brink." *Simulation and Games* 14 (June): 179-200.

Thorngate, W., and B. Carroll. 1987. "Why the Best Person Rarely Wins: Some Embarrassing Facts About Contests." *Simulation and Games* 18 (September): 299-320.

Tucker, A. B. 1986. *Programming Languages* (2nd ed.). New York: McGraw-Hill.

Tuggle, F. D., and F. H. Barron. 1980. "On the Validation of Descriptive Models of Decision-Making." *Acta Psychologica* 45: 197-210.

About the Authors

Lee Sigelman is Dean of Social and Behavioral Sciences and Professor of Political Science, Communication, and Public Administration at the University of Arizona. He has previously served on the faculties of Texas Tech University and the University of Kentucky, and as Director of the Political Science program of the National Science Foundation. His research interests span the fields of American and comparative politics, public administration, and research methodology. He has published in a wide array of social science outlets. His most recent book, coauthored with Susan Welch, is *Blacks' Views of Racial Inequality: The Dream Deferred.*

Marcia Lynn Whicker is a Professor in the Department of Public Administration at Virginia Commonwealth University in Richmond. She holds a Ph.D. in Political Science from the University of Kentucky; master's degrees in economics, political science, and public administration; and an associate degree in electronic engineering technology. She has worked for a variety of government offices, including the Capitol Hill staff of a United States Representative, the United States Senate Budget Committee, the Pennsylvania and South Carolina legislatures, the Comptroller of the Currency, and the Tennessee Valley Authority. Before joining the faculty at Virginia Commonwealth University, she held faculty positions at the University of South Carolina in Columbia, Temple University in Philadelphia, and Wayne State University in Detroit. She has published over 40 professional journal articles, and six books in the areas of public policy, American government, and public administration.

NOTES

NOTES